THE NEGRO LEAGUES

THE STORY OF BLACK BASEBALL

THE NEGRO LEAGUES

THE STORY OF BLACK BASEBALL

JACOB MARGOLIES

THE AFRICAN-AMERICAN EXPERIENCE

FRANKLIN WATTS
NEW YORK   CHICAGO   LONDON   TORONTO   SYDNEY

Y

Photographs copyright ©: National Baseball Library and
Archive, Cooperstown, NY: pp. 1, 2, 3, 4, 6, 10, 12, 13, 14 top,
15; The Bettmann Archive: p. 5; UPI/Bettmann Newsphotos:
pp. 7, 11 bottom; Negro Leagues Baseball Museum, Inc.: pp.8,
9, 11 top; Ap/Wide World Photos: pp. 14 bottom, 16.

Appendix is reprinted from *Only the Ball Was White*,
copyright © 1970 by Robert Peterson.

Library of Congress Cataloging-in-Publication Data

Margolies, Jacob.
The Negro leagues : the story of black baseball/Jacob Margolies.
p. cm.—(An African-American experience)
Appendix reprinted from Only the ball was white/
Robert Peterson. c1970
Includes bibliographical references (p.) and index.
Summary: A history of the Negro Leagues, baseball teams
which flourished in the early twentieth century as a result of
discrimination against black baseball players, and highlight-
ing some of the outstanding players and their achievements.
ISBN 0-531-11130-X
1. Baseball—United States—History—Juvenile literature.
2. Negro leagues—History—Juvenile literature. [1.Negro
leagues—History. 2. Baseball—History. 3. Afro-Americans—
Biography. 4. Baseball players. 5. Discrimination in sports.]
I. Peterson, Robert, 1925– Only the ball was white.
II. Title. III. Series.
GV863.A1M35 1993
793.357'0973—dc20   93-10802 CIP AC

CONTENTS

Introduction
7

I
The Early Years
11

II
The Birth of the Negro Leagues
24

III
The Glory Years
40

IV
In a Foreign Land
66

V
New Horizons
73

VI
After the Color Bar Fell
84

Appendix
93

Source Notes
120

Bibliography
123

Index
124

INTRODUCTION

Since its earliest days nearly 150 years ago, baseball has captured the imagination of Americans. Tales of Babe Ruth's towering blasts, Ty Cobb's daring on the base paths, Joe DiMaggio's grace in the field, and Ted Williams's sweet batting stroke are passed down from generation to generation. The legend and lore of baseball's history give the sport a stature and majesty that other games in the United States lack.

This book tells the story of a part of baseball history that is seldom told. It is a story of great ballplayers who played in obscurity. Because of the color of their skin, these men were not allowed to play on the Yankees or the Dodgers or any other team in Major League baseball. The very existence of these ballplayers was ignored by the great newspapers of their day. Although they performed some of the most remarkable feats baseball has ever known, it was nearly impossible to hear play-by-play coverage of these ballplayers' games on the radio.

In African-American neighborhoods, however, people knew about these players and their teams. In cities across the nation, a world of black baseball existed, separate and apart from the Major Leagues, and flourished for the first half of the twentieth century.

The world of black baseball players in these years contained both triumph and degradation. It was a world in which ballplayers were sometimes asked to play four games in a single day. It was not unusual for a team to spend eight hours traveling by car just to get to a game. Once there, racism often made it impossible for black players to find a hotel that would accept them.

But the world of black baseball was more than hardship and struggle. There were the annual All-Star games, where 50,000 fans would flock to Chicago from all over the nation to see the stars of the game. There were black owners, running their own ball clubs, organizing their own leagues, and bringing entertainment to millions of fans every year.

Most of all there were the players themselves. Jackie Robinson integrated modern-day Major League baseball in 1947, but many great African-American players performed magical feats on baseball diamonds long before the appearance of Robinson. Players like Andrew "Rube" Foster, a great pitcher in his time, but more important, a great strategist, changed the way baseball was played. Foster almost single-handedly organized the first successful Negro league. Cool Papa Bell—perhaps the fastest man ever to play the game—blazed around the bases in 12 seconds flat. The longest home run ever hit at Yankee Stadium was not hit by Babe Ruth or Lou Gehrig or Mickey Mantle, but by Josh Gibson in a Negro League game. According to many, the most electrifying player of his era was the great pitcher Satchel Paige, who had blazing speed accompanied by an unequaled repertoire of pitches. In some games, Paige would actually call his fielders in and tell them to take a rest; he would then proceed to strike out the batter he was facing.

There were many other outstanding players whose accomplishments, because they were achieved in the Negro Leagues, have been largely ignored. Their story is tied up with the history of this nation, and it begins a long time ago.

THE EARLY YEARS

Baseball was first played in the 1840s in New Jersey and New York City. It does not seem likely that any one person invented the game. Many baseball historians think the game may have developed from an English children's game called "rounders," which uses a bat and ball, and was usually played by girls.

It was during the Civil War years (1861–1865) that baseball began to spread rapidly across the nation. The war brought people from all over the United States into close contact. A baseball match between teams from the 165th New York Volunteer Infantry in Hilton Head was watched by some 40,000 soldiers. The game was played in many military camps, and was introduced to new areas by soldiers returning home from the war. By the late 1860s, there were baseball teams all over the country, and the first professional teams were beginning to form.

Although racial prejudice was strong in the early years of professional baseball, social codes were not as rigid as they would later become. In fact, during these early years, a number of African-American ballplayers managed to play alongside whites in some of the top professional leagues in the country.

The first African-American to play Major League baseball was Moses Fleetwood Walker. After graduating from Oberlin College in Ohio, Walker played during 1884 for the Toledo team in the American Association, one of the two major leagues of the day. Walker, a player of only average talents, played professional ball through 1890. Because of his race, he faced constant abuse from fans, teammates, and opponents.

Only a handful of black players were given an opportunity to play in high-level professional leagues in the nineteenth century. Their best chance to show their talents playing alongside whites came in the late 1880s. Some of the best African-American players from baseball's early integrated days were Bud Fowler, who played for dozens of teams all across the United States; pitcher George Stovey, who played for Jersey City in the Eastern League and later for Newark in the International League; and Frank Grant, most notably the star of the Buffalo team in the International League.

Fowler was born in Cooperstown, New York, home of baseball's Hall of Fame. His best position was second base, but he was also a fine pitcher. He played in 1884 for the Stillwater, Minnesota, team in the Northwestern League, one of the top leagues of that time. Fowler was forced off several of the teams he played for by white teammates who did not want to play on the same field with a black man.

George Stovey, a tall left-hander, won thirty-three games for Newark in 1887. He was talented enough to pitch for any team in the country. In 1887, Stovey was scheduled to pitch against Cap Anson's Chicago White Stockings. Anson was the most popular ballplayer of his day. At the last minute, it was announced that Stovey was sick and could not pitch. In actuality, Anson had said he and his team would refuse to play Newark if Stovey, a black man, was allowed to play.

Frank Grant played second base and batted .366 while stealing forty bases for the Buffalo Bisons in 1887, but his teammates refused to sit with him for the team photo in 1888. An 1889 story from the *Sporting News* describes some of what Grant had to put up with:

"Why, the runners chased him [Grant] off second base. They went down so often trying to break his legs or injure him that he gave up his infield position the latter part of last season and played right field. That is not all.

"About half the pitchers try their best to hit these colored players when [they are] at the bat. I know of a great many pitchers that tried to soak Grant. . . . One of the International League pitchers pitched for Grant's head all the time."[1]

Although he hit .326 in the 1888 season, the Buffalo team refused to offer Grant a contract for the new season. Grant played the next three years for a team in Pennsylvania. After 1892, he never again played on a white team.

In the last decade of the nineteenth century, the various leagues gradually pushed African-Americans out of organized professional baseball. Some leagues actually adopted resolutions barring blacks from the game, but more often an unspoken understanding arose that teams were to be kept all-white. These "gentlemen's agreements" would keep Major League baseball a white man's game until

Jackie Robinson integrated the sport some fifty-odd years later.

By the turn of the century, baseball had become America's national game, a powerful force in uniting the different regions of the nation. A prejudiced society and narrow-minded baseball establishment could keep blacks from playing alongside whites, but they could not stop blacks from playing baseball. Concentrated at first on the East Coast, all-black teams were established; the best of them were the equal of any white team. The era of black baseball had begun.

BLACK BASEBALL: THE FIRST TEAMS

There were black baseball teams playing as early as the 1860s. The first black professional team of note was the Cuban Giants, formed in the 1880s and playing out of Trenton, New Jersey. The players were African-American, not Cuban. They may have chosen their name to make themselves seem foreign and exotic and escape some of the prejudice faced by blacks native to the United States.

Among the Cubans' top players was Frank Grant, who had starred for Buffalo before being forced off the team. Another player was the infielder Sol White. One of the main reasons people know about this early chapter of baseball history at all is because White wrote about it in 1906 in his *The History of Colored Baseball*. In 1887, the Cuban Giants played an exhibition game against the Detroit Tigers, winners of a World Series and considered baseball's world champions. The Giants led the game going into the eighth inning before eventually losing to the Tigers.

Other excellent black players joined together to form their own teams. The best clubs were in New

York City, Philadelphia, and Chicago. Although at the turn of the century most blacks still lived in the South, tens of thousands were heading north every year looking for better economic opportunities and hoping to escape the strict and pervasive racial oppression that still existed below the Mason-Dixon line. The most successful teams arose in cities with African-American communities who had the economic means to support them.

Sol White helped organize the Philadelphia Giants, the best team at the turn of the century. Many of the top black clubs in the early twentieth century went by the name the Giants, perhaps because of the popularity of the Major League New York Giants. The Philadelphia team played a competitive two-game exhibition in 1902 against the Majors' American League champion, the Philadelphia Athletics. In 1903, the Philadelphia Giants had a great young pitcher, Rube Foster, who would in later years become the dominant figure in the development of organized professional black baseball.

The Philadelphia Giants star second baseman in 1903 was Charlie Grant. Despite the color of his skin, Grant had come close to playing for the Baltimore Orioles in 1901. The team's manager, John McGraw, was so impressed with Grant's talents that he was determined to sign him to a contract despite the understanding that blacks were not welcome in the Major Leagues. McGraw declared that Grant was actually a Cherokee Indian and said his name was Charlie Tokohama. McGraw's ruse did not work. The Chicago White Sox owner Charlie Comiskey protested "that the Cherokee of McGraw's is really Grant, the crack Negro second baseman . . . fixed up with war paint and a bunch of feathers." Facing pressure from the rest of the American League, McGraw gave up on signing Grant.[2]

The best team during this early period was the Lincoln Giants. They played in the Bronx at the Dyckman Oval in New York City. The Lincoln Giants had two outstanding pitchers, Smokey Joe Williams and Cannonball Dick Redding. Williams, who hailed from Texas, shut out Major League teams several times. In 1917, he pitched a ten-inning no-hitter and struck out twenty batters against the National League champion New York Giants. In center field was Spotswood Poles, a great line-drive hitter and superb base stealer. Behind the plate was another Texan, the huge Louis Santop. Standing six feet four inches (1.9 m), weighing 240 pounds (108 kg), and playing in an era when the baseball was heavier than the livelier ball used today, Santop was known for slugging tremendous home runs. Some of his clouts are supposed to have traveled 500 feet (150 m).

The star of the Lincoln Giants team was John Henry Lloyd, who joined the team in 1911. Lloyd may have been the finest shortstop ever to have played the game. Honus Wagner of the Pittsburgh Pirates, the best Major League shortstop of that era, was once asked who had been the best player in baseball history. Wagner replied, "If you mean who in organized baseball my answer would be Babe Ruth; but if you mean in all baseball, organized or unorganized, the answer would have to be a colored man named John Henry Lloyd."[3] Babe Ruth himself is also supposed to have said that Lloyd was the greatest player he had ever seen.

Lloyd had long arms, huge hands, and was a superb fielder. Against top competition, he regularly hit around .400. In addition to starring on the field, Lloyd managed the Lincoln Giants after Sol White left the position in 1911.

Baseball in these early days was a rough game. Fighting between teams and among players was common. So were beanballs. Lloyd was noted for being a gentleman. His harshest expressions, reserved for occasions when he was truly angry, were "gosh bob it" and "dad gum it."

As one of the highest-paid black ballplayers of his day, Lloyd probably received a salary of about $200 a month, which was a decent salary for the time. Unlike the situation today, salaries in baseball's early days were low. White Major Leaguers were paid better than their black contemporaries, but they certainly were not getting rich from playing baseball.

In addition to playing against each other, during these early years the top black teams traveled from town to town on barnstorming tours, taking on all challengers. They also played college teams, and on rare occasions the Major League clubs. A team might play 100 games in a year. Black baseball was still not organized in a formal league structure, and it was not uncommon for teams to fold during the year and for new teams to form in the middle of a season.

CUBA

Looking to earn more money, many of the best players in the country, black and white, played in Cuba in the fall and winter. Without this chance to earn a salary through the entire year, many of the ballplayers of the day would have had to give up playing baseball. Racial segregation was not as common in Cuba as in the United States, and the baseball teams there generally had both blacks and whites on them.

Cuban baseball gave blacks the chance to play with and against top Major League talent over an extended period of time. Although some Major League owners contended that blacks were not playing in their league because they were not talented enough, the performance of black ballplayers against Major League competition in Cuba disproved that argument.

John Henry Lloyd starred for the Havana Reds, a top Cuban team. At the end of the 1909 baseball season in the United States, the Detroit Tigers of the American League traveled to Cuba and played an eleven-game series against the Reds, losing seven games. Seeking revenge, the Tigers returned to Cuba in 1910, led by Ty Cobb. Aside from Babe Ruth, Cobb was probably the best Major League hitter in the first half of the twentieth century; he was far and away its best base stealer.

Cobb, nicknamed the Georgia Peach, had been the American League batting champion during 1909, with a .385 batting average. He missed the first two of the seven-game series but played in the next five. Cobb hit well over the next five games, but when he tried to steal he had a surprise.

Cobb was one of the meanest players of his day. He wore cleats with sharpened spikes, which he used to cut up the legs of the fielder at second base. Cobb especially disliked blacks, and on his first steal attempt against the Havana Reds he slid into the base with his spikes high. Lloyd had prepared for this. The shortstop was wearing cast-iron shin guards under his baseball stockings. Lloyd took the throw from the Havana team's African-American catcher, Bruce Petway, tagged Cobb out at second base, and sent the Georgia Peach flying as he slid smack into Lloyd's shin guards. Cobb tried to steal two more times, and was thrown out both times. After his third unsuccessful attempt, Cobb ran off the field cursing and swore that he would never again play against blacks. Although the Tigers won six of the seven games, Lloyd had 11 hits in 22 at bats in the series, batting .500. Cobb hit .369.[4]

One of black baseball's early great pitchers was the slender Cuban fastballer José Mendez. After the Major League teams signed two light-skinned Cubans in 1911, there were hopes that the color barrier was breaking down. Mendez, however, was ignored. The white Cuban pitcher Aldolfo Luque would win nearly 200 games in the Major Leagues, and was treated as a hero when he returned to Cuba for winter ball. Mendez would play in the United States for several top black teams, and near the end of his career in the newly formed Negro Leagues, but he would never receive the opportunities afforded his lighter-skinned countrymen.

CHICAGO BASEBALL: INTRODUCING MR. FOSTER

Baseball's popularity grew rapidly between 1900 and 1920. During this period, a number of top-flight black ball clubs sprang up in the Midwest to challenge the supremacy of the Lincoln Giants. Chicago, in particular, became a center for black baseball. Some of the top teams in the region were the Chicago Union Giants, the Indianapolis ABCs, the Leland Giants, and later the Chicago American Giants. It was not uncommon for the top teams to draw over 15,000 fans in a weekend game in Chicago. The growing success of black baseball in Chicago during this period was largely due to the effort and genius of Andrew "Rube" Foster.

Rube Foster was a great pitcher, an innovative teacher and manager, a shrewd businessman, and a superb organizer. He is often referred to as the father of black baseball.

Foster, the son of a minister, was born Andrew

Foster in Calvert, Texas, in 1879. He ran away from home at the age of fourteen to make his life in baseball, and joined the Fort Worth team. As a very young man, he had the chance to pitch against Major League teams who spent their spring training in Texas. Before settling in Chicago, Foster established himself as a dominant force on the East Coast. In 1903, Foster joined the Cuban X Giants, who were then playing out of Philadelphia. It was during the 1902 season that he pitched and beat the great Rube Waddell of the Philadelphia Athletics.[5] At the time, Waddell was the best pitcher in the American League, and from then on, Foster went by the name Rube Foster.

Foster was a very large man at six feet four inches (1.9 m) and 220 pounds (100 kg). He had an excellent fastball, but what made him a great pitcher was his cunning. He mastered a series of other pitches, including a curveball and a fadeaway pitch, or screwball. Foster also liked to throw a submarine pitch, releasing the ball from under his waist. He knew how to confuse batters by changing the speeds of his pitches, and he employed many tricks to annoy batters. Foster said that when the bases were loaded, the pitcher "should smile often . . . this seems to unnerve [the batter] . . . In other instances where the batter appears anxious to hit, waste a little time on him . . . everybody's yelling for him to hit it out, waste a few balls and try his nerve; the majority of times you will win out by drawing him into hitting at a wide one."[6]

In 1903, the X Giants challenged Sol White's Philadelphia Giants to determine the championship in black baseball. The X Giants won the series five games to two, and Foster was the winning pitcher in four of those victories. The following year, Foster switched his allegiances and joined the Philadelphia

Giants. The two teams met again in 1904 in a three-game series. This time, Foster's new team was the victor, and Rube was the winning pitcher in both victories.

Foster's wizardry did not go unnoticed by his white contemporaries. John McGraw, then the manager of the National League's New York Giants, was a great admirer of Foster's. In 1903, he had Rube teach Christy Mathewson the fadeaway pitch. That year, Mathewson won thirty-four games, more than doubling the fourteen he had won the previous year.

Rube went to Chicago in 1906, joining the Leland Giants. He took the best players of the Philadelphia Giants, including Grant "Home Run" Johnson, with him. Outraged over how little money the team was making, Foster persuaded Frank Leland, owner of the Leland Giants, to allow him to do the booking for the club. He demanded that the team receive a fifty-fifty split of the paid attendance for all games, and the team's financial picture brightened rapidly.

The Leland Giants, led by Foster, immediately established themselves as one of the top black teams in America. In 1907 they won 110 games and lost 10. The team continued to dominate the competition over the next few years. John Henry Lloyd, catcher Bruce Petaway, and pitcher Pat Dougherty were among the best players on Foster's team. In 1910, Foster broke away from Frank Leland. He managed the team, which kept the name the Leland Giants, for the season.

In 1911, Foster formed his own team, the Chicago American Giants with many of the same players. Foster's business partner was John Schorling, a white Chicago bar owner who was the brother-in-law of the Chicago White Sox owner Charles Comiskey. The White Sox had just moved into a new ballpark, and Foster's team moved into the old White Sox ballpark. The two men agreed to a fifty-fifty split of all the money they took in, and remained partners for the rest of Foster's days in baseball.

The Chicago American Giants would dominate baseball in the Midwest for many years to come. Foster's players were all well paid, they had the best equipment, and the team traveled by train in their own private Pullman car. This was considered the height of luxury. Foster required his players to follow a strict dress code, and the team projected an impressive dignity. When Foster took his team down South, local whites accustomed to strict segregation were astonished by the sight of successful black men traveling in their own private train car. The team toured all over the United States, often playing in California during the winter months. In 1916, Foster took the team to Cuba to play.

Foster was still occasionally pitching for the Chicago American Giants in 1916, but his career as a player was winding down. As a manager, though, he still controlled the American Giants' games. Foster's approach to the game was revolutionary. His team played an exciting style of baseball that was quite different from the way the game was played in the all-white Major Leagues. Foster always emphasized speed over power. He loved to use the bunt, and he had his players stealing bases at every opportunity. He controlled his pitchers closely. Using signals from the dugout, Foster called every pitch they threw.

The hit-and-bunt was one of Foster's specialties. If the American Giants had a base runner on first, Foster liked to have him take off for second on the pitch. The batter would bunt the ball down the third base line, and the runner who had been on first would dash all the way to third as the fielders made the play on the batter at first. Once, in a game against the

Indianapolis ABCs, Foster had his players bunt successfully eleven times in a row.[7]

Foster was rigorous in preparing his players. His team would spend hours practicing bunting into a hat and a marked-off circle on the infield. One of Foster's best players was third baseman "Gentleman" Dave Malarcher, who earned his nickname due to the fact that he never argued with an umpire and never drank whiskey or smoked a cigarette. Malarcher was fast and smart and had been a star player in the New Orleans area before coming to the American Giants. He was fighting in France during World War I when he received a letter from Foster asking him to join the American Giants after he finished his army service. Malarcher, who eventually succeeded Foster as the team's manager, remembers Foster as "the greatest baseball man who ever lived . . . a great trainer [who] could teach players how to execute and how to develop their abilities."[8]

Second baseman Bingo Demoss was another one of Foster's top players. Like Malarcher, he had great speed and was a terrific base runner and fielder. The only power hitter on the American Giants in the 1920s was the Cuban Christobel Torriente. After the other American Giants had exhausted the opposing pitcher, it was not unusual for Torriente to clear the bases with a long home run.

The pipe-smoking Foster addressed almost everybody he knew as "darling." He usually treated his younger players gently, but he had a temper. Foster was known to give a player who ignored or disregarded his instructions a hard rap across the head with his pipe. The Chicago American Giant players never forgot who was in charge.

THE BIRTH OF THE NEGRO LEAGUES

By the end of World War I, the top white semi-professional teams the American Giants played in the Chicago area were becoming less popular. In 1919, race riots broke out across the United States, with some of the worst in Chicago. The return of Foster's team to Chicago that year was delayed as National Guard troops camped out in the American Giants stadium.

The successful black teams in the region, with the encouragement of Foster, began to think about forming their own league. Foster wrote in his column for the *Chicago Defender*, one of the nation's leading black newspapers, that a Negro league would help keep players' salaries down by making it illegal for teams to steal each other's best players. A league could also determine a championship team that might be able to challenge the Major League champion.

On February 13, 1920, owners of the top Midwest black clubs met at a YMCA in Kansas City. They agreed to establish an eight-team league made up of the American Giants, St. Louis Stars, Kansas City Monarchs, Detroit Stars, Indianapolis ABCs, Cuban Stars (most of whose players actually were Cuban), Chicago Giants, and Dayton Marcos. The owners named it the Negro National League, and it marked the birth of the Negro Leagues. The following year two East Coast teams, the Atlantic City Bacharach Giants and Philadelphia Hilldale Athletics, were made associate members of the league. The two East Coast clubs would occasionally play games against the other teams in the league, when scheduling and travel costs allowed.

Foster wanted blacks to have control of the finances of the new league, and except for the Kansas City Monarchs' J. L. Wilkinson, all the owners of the Negro National League teams were black.

Right away the league was fairly successful. Crowds of 10,000 were not uncommon for weekend games. A major problem the new league faced was that many of the teams did not have their own ballparks and depended on renting stadiums owned by the white professional teams. Foster was the league's president and secretary. He did the scheduling and even helped finance some of the weaker teams. Foster also arranged for some of his top players to join other teams to make sure that they could be competitive with the American Giants.

The Indianapolis ABCs were most fortunate to get Oscar Charleston from the American Giants. Many Negro League old-timers believed that Charleston was the greatest player in the history of the Negro Leagues. He was a terrific outfielder, a powerful hitter, and although he was stocky, had tremendous speed.

Charleston was a fierce competitor, and many players of his day were struck by his cold, penetrating eyes. Charleston also loved to fight. Once during a game against a collection of white Major Leaguers on a barnstorming tour, Charleston became so enraged at an umpire that he knocked him out cold. A near riot ensued, and Charleston was arrested by police. Another time while in the South, Charleston ripped off the mask of a Ku Klux Klan member who confronted him. While playing in Cuba, Charleston, after beating up the opposing team's shortstop and second baseman, took on a number of Cuban soldiers who rushed onto the field to challenge him before he was finally arrested.[1]

Charleston was originally from Indianapolis, and he had played for the ABCs from 1915 to 1919 before joining Foster's Giants. After rejoining the ABCs for the Negro National League's first season, Charleston hit .366. Charleston would have a long career and play for several different teams. He also had great success batting against white Major League pitchers in barnstorming games and in Cuba during the off-season. Charleston hit home runs against Hall of Fame pitchers Walter Johnson and Lefty Grove. Late in his career, Charleston would play first base and manage the Pittsburgh Crawfords, which some people think was the greatest baseball team that ever played the game.

Following the example of Foster, the best East Coast teams formed the Eastern Colored League in 1923. During its first season, the league's six teams were the Baltimore Black Sox, Hilldale Athletics from Philadelphia, New York's Lincoln Giants, Cuban Stars (also of New York), Brooklyn Royal Giants, and Bacharach Giants (who played out of Atlantic City and were named after their sponsor, the city's mayor, Harry Bacharach). The two best teams during the Eastern Colored League's history were Hilldale and the Bacharach Giants. The league was more loosely organized than Foster's Negro National

League. Teams still played most of their games outside the league, barnstorming against semiprofessional teams throughout the region. Unlike Foster's league, most of the owners of the Eastern Colored League were white. The Hilldale Athletics' Ed Bolen and the Cuban Stars' Alex Pompez were the only black owners.

With the establishment of two distinct leagues, it would now be possible to have the first organized black world series. Foster did not get along with the East Coast owners and blamed them for raiding players from the Negro National League, but in spite of their differences, the two leagues' champion teams agreed to meet in 1924.

The Kansas City Monarchs faced off against the Hilldale Athletics. The Hilldale team was led by their catcher, Biz Mackey, and a young third baseman, Judy Johnson, who would star in the Negro Leagues for many years to come. Mackey was a master behind the plate. Pitchers loved having Mackey as their catcher. He had a very powerful throwing arm and got rid of the ball so quickly that time after time, base runners trying to steal found themselves thrown out. Judy Johnson was a terrific hitter and one of the best fielders of his era. He had a strong arm, great range, and knew how to position himself for different batters.

Kansas City was led by "Bullet" Joe Rogan. Rogan was one of the best fastball pitchers in baseball history; he also threw an excellent curveball. And Rogan was not just a pitcher, he was also a fine hitter.

In the ten-game 1924 Negro League world series between Hilldale and Kansas City, Rogan pitched four of the games, winning two and losing one. He also played center field in the other six games and batted .325 for the series. The series was tied four games apiece with one tie game. In the final game, the great Cuban pitcher José Mendez came out to pitch for the Monarchs. The aging Mendez, forty years old and manager of the Kansas City team, pitched a shutout and Kansas City won the deciding game 5–0.[2]

The following year Hilldale would win the Negro Leagues world series, and in 1926 and 1927, the Chicago American Giants were the champions of black baseball.

CLOSING THE DOOR ON MAJOR LEAGUE VERSUS NEGRO LEAGUE CONTESTS

While organized black ball was thriving, white professional baseball was going through important changes. The Major League owners had chosen a new commissioner, Judge Kenesaw Mountain Landis, who was asserting his strong control over the game. During the 1919 Major League World Series, a group of players on the Chicago White Sox were paid by gamblers to lose games. The resulting scandal frightened the owners, who feared that angry fans would desert the game. Hoping to restore the public's confidence, in 1920 the owners appointed Landis, who prior to his selection had been a federal judge. He was given the power to run the game as he saw fit, and for the next twenty-four years Landis was Major League baseball's commissioner.

The Negro League ballplayers have bitter memories of Landis. The commissioner would not allow Major League teams to play black teams. Before Landis, these games had been very popular and were big money-makers for the top black clubs. Landis could not completely prevent Major League ballplayers from forming their own touring squads in the off-season, but he would not allow them to wear their Major League team uniforms. On several occasions Landis did succeed in canceling all-star contests between Major League and Negro League stars. When Rube Foster met with Landis to complain about the unfair new policy, Landis reportedly replied, "Mr. Foster, when you beat our teams, it gives us a black eye."

Landis did not speak publicly on the subject, but those who remember him say that he was determined to keep the Major League game all-white. Some black players blame Landis for keeping them out of the so-called big leagues, but the truth is that nearly all the Major League owners were opposed to integrating the game.

Racist attitudes and segregation were so ingrained in much of America during the first half of the twentieth century that few whites actually thought about the injustice of baseball's color bar. Unlike today, there were no federal laws in the United States that prohibited racial discrimination in employment. In the South, segregation, which prohibited blacks from schools, restaurants, hotels, and bathrooms that whites used, was the law of the land. But even in the North, many hotels and restaurants would not serve blacks. Many large corporations had unwritten policies against hiring blacks for anything other than the lowliest positions. Even the United States Army was segregated. The fact that blacks were not allowed to play in the Major Leagues was not at all unusual when you consider that period in history.

TAKING ROOT

Shortly after Foster helped set up the Negro National League, a sort of minor league circuit for black players developed in the South. As most of the nation's blacks still lived in that part of the United States, this was not surprising. Nashville, Atlanta, New Orleans, Jacksonville, and Birmingham all had successful teams.

Segregation was much more rigid in the South than in the rest of the nation. The widespread poverty of the region, along with the prohibition against interracial games, made it impossible for these teams to support their players in a style similar to that of teams in the North. Many of the Southern Negro League teams could not even afford to provide lodgings for their players when they were on the road, and the salaries were very low, usually less than fifty dollars a month.

Despite the hardships, many of the legends of the Negro Leagues started out playing in the Southern Negro League. When the top teams from the Northeast and Midwest had their spring training and early-season barnstorming games down South, they also looked to pick up young players from the southern teams. Satchel Paige, the most famous Negro League player of all time, got his start playing for the Chattanooga team in the Southern Negro League. Later on, another minor league circuit for black baseball would develop in Texas and Oklahoma.

In 1926, organized black baseball suffered a serious blow when Rube Foster had a mental breakdown. Perhaps the stress and pressure of running a league and managing his team finally became too much. Foster began hallucinating. While in his apartment, he began imagining he saw fly balls along Madison Avenue. Foster also had a recurring vision that he was needed to pitch in a World Series game. Foster's wife finally had him committed to the state insane asylum at Kankakee, Illinois, and Dave Malarcher took over managing the Chicago

American Giants. Foster spent the final four years of his life at Kankakee. He died on December 9, 1930.

Under Foster's leadership, baseball had become the most popular game in the black community. At his funeral, more than 3,000 people stood for hours in pouring rain and snow. Among the impressive floral displays was a 200-pound (90-kg) arrangement of white chrysanthemums in the shape of baseballs, with red roses for the balls' seams, donated by the National Negro League owners. A long procession followed Foster's casket to Lincoln Cemetery.[3]

Foster had succeeded in establishing baseball as an institution in the African-American community. Although his league would suffer its demise during the Great Depression, black organized baseball would be part of the American landscape until the Major Leagues were finally integrated.

THE SPIRIT OF ST. LOUIS

Along with the Kansas City Monarchs and Chicago American Giants, a third team dominated the Negro National League in its early years. The St. Louis Stars were not as well known as some other top teams, but they won several league championships.

The Stars were led by James "Cool Papa" Bell. When Bell started playing for the Stars in 1922, he was only nineteen years old. Impressed that the young man was not nervous before big crowds, his teammates started calling him Cool Papa.

The great pitcher Satchel Paige was only exaggerating slightly when he said that Cool Papa Bell was so fast that he could turn off the light switch, and then jump into bed before the light went off. Bell could circle the four bases in twelve seconds flat. It was not uncommon for him to go from first to third base when the batter at the plate bunted. When on base, Bell was a master at studying the pitcher so that he could get as large a lead as possible. He knew all the baserunning tricks. Bell would always touch the inside part of the base with his foot when circling the bases so that he could travel the least possible distance to get where he needed to go.[4] In 1933, Bell stole 175 bases, a record that has never been equaled.

Bell was also a terrific batter. He hit over .400 several times in his career. He played for the Stars for ten years, mostly as an outfielder, and his team won the Negro National League championship in three of those ten years.

Cool Papa Bell played Negro League ball until 1946. In addition to playing for the Stars in the 1920s, he played for the great Pittsburgh Crawfords in the 1930s, and the Homestead Grays in the 1940s. All three teams were National Negro League champions, thanks in large part to Cool Papa's hitting and baserunning.

Along with Bell's speed, St. Louis had the power of the huge Mule Suttles, one of the leading home-run hitters in the history of the Negro Leagues. When Suttles came to the plate, the fans would chant, "Kick, Mule, kick!" Teammates who saw him play say that some of Suttles's home runs easily traveled 500 feet (150 m).

A third all-time great on the St. Louis team was the shortstop Willie Wells. Like Cool Papa Bell and Suttles, Wells had a long career in the Negro Leagues that continued for many years after he left the Stars. From 1923 until 1931, when the St. Louis Stars disbanded, Wells sparkled as the team's shortstop. Wells was only five feet seven inches (1.7 m) tall, but he was strong and hit for a high average. In

1929, he hit twenty-seven home runs—more than Suttles—to lead the Negro National League. Wells was also a smooth fielder, continuing in the tradition of John Henry Lloyd. With Bell, Suttles, and Wells, the St. Louis team was among the top teams in Negro League ball in the 1920s.

BACK EAST

In addition to the Bacharach and Hilldale teams of the Eastern Colored League, there was another great black baseball team in the 1920s, the Homestead Grays. (Homestead was a suburb of Pittsburgh.) The owner of the team, Cumberland Posey, was light skinned and was often mistaken for white, but his grandfather had been a slave. His father was successful in business and owned a fleet of coal barges as well as being involved in banking and real estate.[5]

Players remember Cum Posey as one of the more generous owners of his day. Posey kept his team out of the Eastern Colored League because it was able to make more money as an independent, traveling over the East Coast and taking on all challengers.

The Homestead Grays beat the best teams in the region, including the Hilldale Athletics, and won several games against white Major League all-star squads. They played many of their games at Forbes Field when the Major League Pittsburgh Pirates were out of town. The early Grays teams featured the spitball pitcher Sam Streeter, the legendary Smokey Joe Williams (who had previously pitched for the Lincoln Giants), and the second baseman George Scales.

The Bacharach Giants won the Eastern Colored League championship in 1926 and 1927. They had one of the finest infields in the history of the Negro Leagues, anchored by Dick Lundy and Oliver "Ghost" Marcelle. The shortstop, Dick Lundy, was nearly as good as John Henry Lloyd had been at that position in his prime. The soft-spoken Lundy had a strong throwing arm and could snare any ball hit near him. He also managed the team.

Hailing from New Orleans was the great third baseman Oliver Marcelle, who may have been the best fielding player of his era. He also regularly hit over .300. The hot-tempered Marcelle was constantly getting into brawls. His career was ended prematurely when his nose was bitten off during a ferocious fight with a teammate while playing in Cuba.

BASEBALL'S AMBASSADORS

Black ball clubs traveled across America and all over the world. Early in the century, the United States was more a nation of farming communities and small towns than it is today. The Kansas City Monarchs regularly traveled through Wisconsin and Minnesota to play local teams. The Chicago American Giants and Homestead Grays barnstormed through Canada. In some towns where the clubs played, many of the local people had never before come into contact with blacks.

Teams got to a game in many different ways. While the most well off teams traveled by train, players usually got from one town to another crowded together in a car or in old buses. In some cases, players depended on farm wagons and carts pulled by horses to reach their destinations. Barnstorming players slept in cars, buses, rooming houses, and in some cases on the side of the road or in the railroad station. During the 1930s, the Kansas

City Monarchs would often camp out in tents at road sites during their barnstorming tours. Satchel Paige, who barnstormed for over twenty years, remembers that he and his teammates "would travel all night and play ball the next day. We might sleep two or three nights a week."

Even in later years, the successful teams often had to travel under less than ideal conditions. Judy Johnson remembers that it was not unusual to have nine players in a single car. If a team was lucky enough to have a bus, the players often did the driving. Racism and segregation made life on the road even more difficult. It was often impossible to find a restaurant willing to serve blacks, and the players had to eat their meals on the bus. Black ballplayers became very accustomed to sandwiches, sardines, and whatever else was easy to eat while riding in a bus.

Life on the road was rough. Compared to today's Major League players, who fly first class, stay in luxury hotels, and make millions of dollars, the conditions for black players barnstorming across the continent were brutal. While the better Negro League ballplayers during the 1920s earned about $250 a month, a very good salary for that time, the pace was exhausting. If the players had not loved the game, few would have been able to tolerate the constant travel that was a part of black baseball.

Some of the barnstorming black teams looked upon their touring as show business, and the players performed comedy routines before and sometimes during the game. Infielders would throw the ball around the baseball diamond faster and faster until they finally threw away the ball and went through the same motion without the ball. (The Harlem Globetrotters basketball team would later adopt a similar shadow ball routine.)

During the later days of Negro League baseball, a few teams developed extensive "clowning" routines. The Indianapolis Clowns' catcher played behind home plate sitting in a rocking chair. Their first baseman sometimes wore a dress and a four-foot (1.2-m)-long fielding glove. The Clowns also had two comics—Spec Bebop, a dwarf, and King Tut, who dressed in a tuxedo and top hat. They performed skits between innings. A lot of the Negro League players looked down on "clowning" because they thought it distracted from the game and was demeaning to the players. There was no place for clowning in actual Negro League matches and, although many people remember teams like the Clowns, it is only an aside to the history of black baseball.[6]

Black ball clubs did not play only in North America. In 1927, a group of black all-stars went to Japan for a series of games. Most Japanese today think Babe Ruth and Lou Gehrig introduced professional baseball to Japan in 1934. But it was actually the 1927 tour by Negro League players, which included stars like Biz Mackey and Ted Page, and was extremely successful. Some of the games were played in the new Meiji Shrine Stadium in Tokyo, and the city's mayor threw out the first ball. In 1934, members of the Kansas City Monarchs went on a thirteen-month tour of the Orient, playing in Japan, Hawaii, Hong Kong, and the Philippines. Today, baseball is Japan's most popular sport. The Negro League ballplayers deserve much credit for introducing and popularizing baseball in Japan.

Black ballplayers also had the opportunity to play extensively throughout Latin America. In addition to Cuba, African-Americans played important roles in the history of baseball in Puerto Rico, the Dominican Republic, and Mexico. Wherever baseball was played in the world during the first half of the twentieth century, the influence of Negro League ballplayers can be seen. They served as worthy ambassadors for America's national pastime.

HARD TIMES

Most businesses did well in the 1920s, but although industry was producing more and more goods, workers' pay was increasing only very slowly. Unlike industry, farmers suffered terrible difficulties throughout the 1920s, and by the latter part of the decade, many farmers were so in debt they were losing their land.

Even during the 1920s, when the economy was relatively strong, the Negro National Leagues and Eastern Colored League were fragile organizations. The number of league games varied every year. In the Negro National League, the season was generally about eighty games. After 1925, the league split its season into two parts, and the winner of the first half played the winner of the second half to determine the league champion. In the more loosely structured Eastern Colored League, the season was even shorter, usually between fifty and seventy games. The financial condition of the weaker teams in both leagues was always suspect. The poorest teams often folded at the end of the season and, in a couple of cases, teams even went out of business in the middle of the season.

It is not surprising that the leagues had difficulties. Blacks made up only about 10 percent of America's population, and most blacks still lived in the South. Consequently, the number of fans who could be depended upon to support the Negro League teams, which were concentrated in the East Coast and the Midwest, was much smaller than the white population supporting the Major League teams. And in a nation that was still mostly segregated, the poorer black community faced economic disadvantages that made it difficult to provide constant support for the Negro League teams.

In 1928, as the owners quarreled among themselves, the Eastern Colored League folded in the spring. The following year, the league re-formed under the name of the American Negro League; it lasted only for a season. Meanwhile, although it missed the leadership and business skills of its founder Rube Foster, the Negro National League continued to operate fairly smoothly. Eventually, however, even the Negro National League would fall victim to the Great Depression.

In October 1929, stock values on the New York Stock Exchange crashed—banks, businesses, and thousands of people who owned stocks lost huge sums of money. This marked the beginning of the Great Depression. Over the next four years, the economy continued to deteriorate. Thousands of banks failed and went out of business, and millions of people lost their life's savings. By 1933, 25 percent of the nation was out of work. Government welfare programs did not exist as they do today, and millions of Americans had to depend on soup kitchens for food. Times were tough all across the country. (A popular song of the day that illustrated this was "Brother Can You Spare a Dime?")

Black baseball was hit hard by the Great Depression. Some owners were nearly ruined financially, and fans could no longer afford to buy tickets. After the 1931 season, the Negro National League went out of business. For the first time since 1920, there was no functioning Negro League.

Out of the ashes, however, new leagues were

about to arise. The depression would continue through the 1930s but, amazingly, new Negro leagues stronger than their predecessors would develop during these years. These leagues would be led by a new group of powerful and successful African-American owners. The Negro Leagues of the 1930s and 1940s would also be blessed with some of the most fantastic and entertaining players ever to play the game. The new Negro Leagues and these outstanding players would eventually prove so successful that they would topple the racial barriers separating blacks from whites on the nation's ball fields. Baseball's wall of segregation would come tumbling down, and baseball and America would be changed forever.

THE GLORY YEARS

In the 1930s, black baseball's renaissance flowered in an unexpected location—Pittsburgh. As the decade began, the leading black team was Cum Posey's Homestead Grays. Other teams hurt by the Great Depression could not afford to continue paying players the salaries they were accustomed to. Posey was able to entice the great Oscar Charleston and the clutch-hitting and smooth-fielding third baseman Judy Johnson to sign with the Grays. Posey also had a young Pittsburgh local, Josh Gibson, playing catcher. Over the years, Gibson would become known as the greatest home-run hitter in the history of the Negro Leagues. During the 1931 season, when the Grays toured the nation, Josh hit seventy-five home runs.

In 1932, a new owner appeared in Pittsburgh to challenge Posey. Gus Greenlee, nicknamed "Big Red," was intent on putting together the best black baseball team money could buy. The squad Greenlee put together over the next five years was one of the finest baseball teams of all time. That team, the

Pittsburgh Crawfords, has been compared to Babe Ruth and Lou Gehrig's 1927 New York Yankees, often said to be the most powerful Major League team ever.

Gus Greenlee made his fortune running numbers, or on what is known today as the lottery. Today, many states run their own legal lotteries, but during Greenlee's day lotteries were illegal. In most big cities, it was gangsters who ran the numbers operations. An agreed-upon three-digit figure, often based on the last three numbers of the attendance at the local racetrack as shown in the daily newspaper, would be the day's winning number. Anybody could bet, and if you chose the winning figure, you were paid at 500-to-1 odds. A ten-cent bet could win fifty dollars. It was a lucrative business, and it made Greenlee a rich man. Gus also did well hijacking liquor trucks during Prohibition, when alcohol could only be sold illegally. Greenlee operated out of the Crawford Grille, a restaurant and nightclub where many jazz greats, including Duke Ellington, performed.

The contrast between Posey, a legitimate businessman, and Big Red was marked. Greenlee, who was already attempting to promote boxers, decided he wanted a baseball team. He built his own ballpark, the 7,500-seat Greenlee Field, at a cost of $60,000, a huge sum during the Great Depression. Then he went about recruiting players.

Greenlee first had the good fortune to get the extraordinary Satchel Paige, who would become the most famous black ballplayer of his day. He then signed the spitball pitcher Sam Streeter, along with Jimmy Crutchfield. Crutchfield was a tiny man, but he was a fine hitter and one of the best outfielders of the period. Then Greenlee looked at his crosstown rival and started raiding the Homestead Grays.

Posey, who was by now feeling the effect of the depression, did not have the money to compete, and it would be years before his club recovered. Oscar Charleston, Judy Johnson, Josh Gibson, Ted Page, and Ted "Double Duty" Radcliffe all switched over to the Crawfords. The following year, Greenlee picked up Cool Papa Bell, who had led the St. Louis Stars before the team folded during the hard economic times. In 1933, Greenlee also organized a new National Negro League and named himself league president. Eventually, the new league would thrive, and its existence continued until 1948—one year after Jackie Robinson integrated Major League baseball.

Greenlee had assembled a truly awe-inspiring team. He bought a luxurious Mack bus, and the Crawfords were ready to roll. From the beginning, the Crawfords' pitching ace was Satchel Paige. Greenlee had a talent for promotion, and he immediately recognized that Paige had the skill and the charisma to draw fans into the ballpark.

SATCHEL

He was known to many as "the Master"; others called him "the traveling man." He began playing professional ball in the 1920s and was still pitching in the 1960s. Satchel Paige was a storyteller who loved to tell tall tales, but as best as baseball's historians can determine, he pitched in about 2,500 games, had 250 shutouts, and played on 250 different teams. Like Babe Ruth and later Muhammad Ali, Paige had such a magnetic personality that even people who had no interest in sports would come to see him perform.

Leroy "Satchel" Paige was born in Mobile, Alabama. His date of birth remains something of a mystery. Satchel always refused to divulge when he was born, but the general consensus seems to be 1906. He got the name Satchel as a small child because he carried satchels and suitcases while working in the Mobile train station.

Paige was a mischievous child, and in 1918, at the age of twelve, he was sent away to reform school for stealing. Satchel lived there for five years. When he got out, he began playing ball for the Mobile Tigers, a semiprofessional team in his hometown. Eventually, a Negro Southern League team from Chattanooga, Tennessee, signed Paige. From there he went on to the Birmingham Black Barons and later the Baltimore Black Sox. He also played in Cuba. In 1931, Satchel joined Gus Greenlee's new team, the Pittsburgh Crawfords.

Once in Pittsburgh, the skinny six-foot-four-inch (1.9-m) Paige quickly established himself as a dominant pitcher. He had a blazing fastball and pinpoint control. Although he normally threw overhand, Satchel sometimes pitched with a sidearm or submarine motion to baffle the opposition. He had an assortment of trick pitches, including his famous "hesitation pitch," where, in the middle of his pitching motion, Paige would stop for a split second before completing the pitch. He used his blooper, or floater ball, to embarrass hitters. It was his fastball, however, that Paige depended on most. Satchel had many names for his best fastballs, among them Long Tom, thoughtful stuff, bee ball, jump ball, bat dodger, and trouble ball.

Paige believed baseball should be fun. He sometimes had his outfielders and third baseman join him on the mound for a conversation while he pitched to the opposing batter. He usually struck the batter out, much to the fans' delight. Sometimes Satchel would place a gum wrapper over a part of the plate to indicate exactly where he intended to pitch the ball.

Paige was such a drawing card that he was often allowed to travel to games in his own car, separately from the rest of the team. It was not uncommon for him to show up after the game had already begun. In the 1930s, he drove a green Packard convertible that he had bought from the movie star Bette Davis. A story about Paige maintains that he was once stopped for speeding. The judge fined him forty dollars and asked Paige if he had anything to say. Paige took out his wallet, pulled out eighty dollars, and said, "Here you go, judge, because I'm coming back this way tomorrow."

Even off the field Satchel was usually the center of attention. He played several instruments, including the ukulele, loved to sing four-part harmony, and was a top-notch pool player. Many black musicians and entertainers of the period became friends with Paige, enjoying his company when they performed at Greenlee's Crawford Grille.

Paige had a nickname for nearly everybody. Buck O'Neil, a great first baseman for the Kansas City Monarchs during the 1940s and Paige's teammate, was called Nancy, the result of a trip with Satchel. O'Neil remembers that once when the team was on the road, Paige was entertaining two women in different rooms of the hotel. Paige knocked on the door to one room whispering, "Nancy, Nancy?" The other woman opened her door and said, "What's going on, who is this Nancy?" Just then O'Neil opened the door and came out of his room. From that moment on, O'Neil was known as Nancy.[1]

O'Neil remembers Paige fondly, but some of Satchel's teammates resented the attention paid to him. A few thought that his behavior was undignified and some found him arrogant, but the public loved Paige.

Paige was an entertainer, but he was first and

foremost an outstanding pitcher. Pitching for the Crawfords, one of his best years was 1934. At one point in the season, Paige threw four straight shutouts, ending with a no-hitter and seventeen strikeouts in a game against the Homestead Grays. Paige allowed under two runs per game that season.[2]

One of the most memorable confrontations Paige ever had on the mound occurred in 1942. Paige was pitching for the Kansas City Monarchs, the best Negro League team in the Midwest that year. Along with another top pitcher, Hilton Smith, and the sure-hitting first baseman Buck O'Neil, the thirty-six-year-old Paige led the Monarchs. The Monarchs were facing the Homestead Grays, the best Negro League team in the East that year. As usual, the Grays' star slugger Josh Gibson led the Negro Leagues in home runs. Paige was pitching in the seventh inning, with the Monarchs leading 4–0. After getting the first two batters of the inning out, the next batter tripled. Paige called the Monarchs' first baseman Buck O'Neil to the mound and told him he was going to walk the next two batters so that he could pitch to Josh with the bases loaded. O'Neil told Paige he was crazy, but Satchel went ahead and walked the next batter. Then Buck Leonard came up to the plate with Gibson ready on the on-deck circle. Paige yelled out to Gibson that he was going to walk Leonard and that Gibson better get ready. Leonard walked, and the stunned crowd watched as Gibson came up with the bases loaded.

Gibson stepped up to the plate and Satchel yelled to him, "Now, I'm gonna throw you a fastball, but I'm not gonna trick you, I'm gonna give you a fastball." Paige reared back and threw the first ball that Gibson watched for a strike.

Then Paige yelled to Gibson, "Now, I'm gonna throw you another fastball, but I'm not gonna try and trick you. Only it's gonna be a little faster than that other one." Again Paige fired the ball in, and again Gibson did not get the bat off his shoulder. "Strike two," called the umpire.

Paige got the ball back from the catcher and called to Gibson again, "Now, I'm not gonna try to trick you. I'm not gonna throw any smoke around your yoke. I'm gonna throw a pea by your knee, only it's gonna be faster than the first two." Satchel kicked up his leg and let the ball fly. It blazed in and hit the outside part of the plate. The stunned Gibson had struck out and never even gotten to swing the bat.[3]

Paige pitched where the money was. He played from 1937 through 1939 in the Dominican Republic, Mexico, and Puerto Rico. And in 1935, Paige pitched for an integrated semiprofessional team in Bismarck, North Dakota.

By the late 1930s and through the 1940s, Paige had become well known not just to black baseball fans but also to whites. During this time, off-season games between Major League players facing Negro Leaguers started in earnest. The great St. Louis Cardinals pitcher Dizzy Dean organized a Major League touring team that faced off against Negro Leaguers. The pitching battles between Dean and Paige drew much attention to Paige and the Negro League stars. Dean said that Paige was the best pitcher he had ever seen.

In the 1940s, the Cleveland Indian pitcher Bob Feller, who threw faster than any pitcher in the Major Leagues, organized Major League All-Star touring exhibitions against a Negro League squad led by Satchel Paige. These all-star contests proved very lucrative to all the players involved, especially Feller and Paige, who took a percentage of the attendance receipts. The black-white games once again proved to skeptical white sportswriters that blacks could play baseball just as well as whites, and that the two races could meet on the ball field without riots occurring.

During the 1940s, Paige pitched for the Kansas City Monarchs. Satchel was getting old, and by the middle of the decade his Long Tom had lost some of its zip. The Monarchs' other star pitcher, Hilton Smith, often came into games to relieve Paige. Some of the Monarchs thought Smith was now the team's best pitcher. Satchel could still have a great day on the mound from time to time, but it seemed that his career was winding down.

But Paige was still a big drawing card. He was sometimes rented out by the Monarchs owner J. L. Wilkinson, one of the founders of Rube Foster's first Negro National League, to pitch for other teams.

In 1947, baseball fans around the nation focused all their attention on a player named Jackie Robinson, as he became the first black man in the twentieth century to play Major League baseball. Overnight, Satchel and the other Negro Leaguers were virtually forgotten. In 1948, just as Satchel was thinking of retiring, he was offered a contract by the Cleveland Indians. Satchel Paige was about to become a forty-two-year-old Major League rookie.

Cleveland owner Bill Veeck was harshly criticized for signing the aging Paige. The *Sporting News* described Paige's arrival in the Majors as "a publicity stunt" that would "demean the standards of baseball."

The Indians were in a close pennant race, and every game Paige pitched in was important. After a couple of relief appearances and a successful start, Satchel started again against the Chicago White Sox on August 13. The paid attendance for the game was 51,013, the largest night crowd ever to gather at Comiskey Park. Thousands more barged through the turnstiles without paying in order to get a chance to see "the Master" in action. Paige mixed up his trick pitches with a few select Long Toms, and the fans were treated to a three-hit shutout by Paige as the Indians won 5–0. A week later, he faced off against the White Sox again, this time at Cleveland's Municipal Stadium. The crowd for the game in Cleveland was 78,382—the largest number of people to ever attend a night baseball game. Paige again was masterful, and the fans saw another three-hit shutout.[4]

For the year, Paige won six games, lost only one, and saved several. His earned run average was 2.48. When it was suggested to Paige by sportswriters that he should be named rookie of the year, he responded by asking them which year they were talking about. Cleveland won the pennant, but much to Satchel's bitter disappointment the Indians' manager Lou Boudreau did not use him in the World Series.

The ageless Paige kept on pitching. He spent 1951 through 1953 as the top relief pitcher for the American League St. Louis Browns. In 1953, at the age of forty-seven, Satchel pitched an inning for the American League at the All-Star game. Paige had lost his Long Tom, but he was still a better-than-average Major League pitcher. If Paige had been given the opportunity to pitch in the Major Leagues twenty years earlier, when he was in his prime, he would certainly have been recognized as the game's best pitcher.

Paige was a top pitcher for the Triple-A minor league Miami team from 1956 to 1958. Satchel got one last chance to pitch in the Majors at the age of fifty-nine in 1965, when he threw three scoreless innings for the Kansas City A's. This time, Paige's appearance was little more than a publicity stunt, but it did give him an extra year of service for his

Major League pension, and Satchel proved he could still pitch.

Paige gave the following advice to those who might seek to emulate his longevity in baseball: "Avoid running at all times" and "Don't look back. Something may be gaining on you." In 1971, Paige became the first Negro League ballplayer to be admitted to baseball's Hall of Fame in Cooperstown, New York. Satchel Paige, the man who introduced Negro League baseball to all of America, died on June 8, 1982.

THE NEW NEGRO LEAGUES

With the second Negro National League up and running in 1933, a new set of owners moved to make their mark on black baseball. Cum Posey, who had refused to join the new league headed by his rival Gus Greenlee, relented, and in 1935 the Homestead Grays joined the fold. As was the case in the original Negro National League, the teams played a two-part split season, but the new league played fewer games. The number of league games changed every year but was usually only about sixty. Most of the teams were concentrated in the East, but one of the league's better teams, Cole's American Giants (formerly the Chicago American Giants) was from Chicago. The team was owned by the gangster Robert Cole, who took it over shortly after Rube Foster's death.

The United States was still suffering from the effects of the Great Depression, and it was difficult to find owners with the resources to finance a team. Greenlee turned to his associates, who were running numbers rackets in other cities.

Owning a baseball team was a way for the numbers operators to gain status and respectability. It also provided the gangster-owners with a way to hide their money from the tax collector. For that reason, some owners were willing to lose money on a baseball team. But there were also altruistic motives for owning a ball club. After making a fortune from poor people's pennies, many of these new owners felt an obligation to give something back to their community. A topflight professional baseball club could provide entertainment for hundreds of thousands of people each season. The New York Black Yankees, Cuban Stars, Newark Eagles, Baltimore Elite Giants, and Philadelphia Stars were all owned by numbers operators.

The Negro League players and the black community had a fairly tolerant view of the new class of owners. If the players were paid a good wage, they were happy. And in the neighborhoods where they ran their businesses, many people viewed the numbers game as a fairly harmless activity.

A second Negro League, the Negro American League, was organized in 1937, and was made up mainly of teams from the Midwest. The top club in the league was the Kansas City Monarchs. After the original Negro National League had folded, J. L. Wilkinson, the Monarchs' owner, had managed to keep his team operating as an independent club, playing all over the world. By 1937, Wilkinson and other Midwest owners had the resources necessary to establish their own league.

The Negro American League was largely able to avoid the gangster financing that dominated the Negro National League. In addition to the Midwest teams, the Birmingham Barons, a team that had formerly played in the Southern Negro League, joined the new league. Steel mills and other heavy industry had attracted many southern blacks to Birmingham, and although segregation there remained rigid, the black community now had the ability to support an excellent baseball team.

As had been the case in the original Negro National League in the 1920s, players switched teams constantly. It was hard for fans to feel strong loyalty to a team, since teams spent so much of their time barnstorming. Gus Greenlee came up with an idea that he hoped would spark the interest of fans—an East-West All-Star game. The game would become an annual affair, and it almost immediately became the most important event in the world of Negro League baseball.

ALL STARS

The first Major League All-Star game was played at Comiskey Park in 1933. Babe Ruth smacked a home run, and the American League won the game. Later that same year in the same ballpark, the first Negro League East-West game was played. The genius behind the promotion of the game was in allowing the fans to choose who would play. Fans could vote for their favorite players through ballots that appeared in two of the nation's leading black newspapers, the *Chicago Defender* and the *Pittsburgh Courier*. Although both papers covered local news, they were also national newspapers that were read across the country. Still, players from the Pittsburgh and Chicago teams dominated the game in the early years. As the newspapers promoted the game, fan interest was aroused. Voting was extremely heavy. Each year hundreds of thousands of fans cast their ballots.

The game, which was played each year in Chicago from 1933 to 1950, quickly became a major social event in the African-American community. Fans traveled from around the nation to attend. The

Union Pacific Railroad had to add extra cars to its trains to accommodate the many people coming from the South to see the big event. By the 1940s, crowds for the East-West game were between 40,000 and 50,000. Being chosen to play in the All-Star game was the single greatest honor a Negro League player could receive. The All-Stars were put up at the luxurious Grand Hotel and were treated as conquering heroes.

Gentleman Dave Malarcher was not alone in believing that the success of the East-West game was what convinced the Major Leagues to finally integrate the game. Malarcher said that "when the Major Leagues saw 50,000 to 60,000 fans in that ballpark—well Branch Rickey [the Brooklyn Dodger general manager who signed Jackie Robinson] saw he had something more than a little black boy. He had those great crowds. That is what did it. He saw what black fans would do for the pocketbook of the Major Leagues."[5]

The 1934 and 1935 East-West games rank among the most exciting of the series. In 1934, the East team boasted Cool Papa Bell, Oscar Charleston, Jimmy Crutchfield, and Josh Gibson. Leading the West were the shortstop Willie Wells, and the power hitters Mule Suttles and Turkey Stearnes. Willie Foster, Rube Foster's younger brother and one of the great pitchers of the Negro Leagues, was also on the West squad.

The 1934 game was scoreless in the seventh inning when Willie Wells doubled for the West. Satchel Paige was called in from the bullpen to pitch.

First up to face Paige was Ted "Double Duty" Radcliffe. Radcliffe had gotten the name Double Duty after an amazing performance at Yankee Stadium in 1932 against the New York Black Yankees. Playing at that time for the Crawfords, Radcliffe caught the first game of a doubleheader pitched by Satchel Paige. Paige pitched a shutout. In the second game, Radcliffe pitched and threw another shutout for Pittsburgh. The famous New York newspaper writer Damon Runyon was at Yankee Stadium that day. Runyon was so amazed by Radcliffe's endurance and virtuosity that he called him Double Duty in his newspaper column the next day.

Facing Paige in the 1934 East-West game, Radcliffe did not fare so well, as Paige struck him out. Then Satchel got Turkey Stearnes and Mule Suttles to fly out, and Wells was left stranded on second base.

In the eighth inning the East finally got on the scoreboard, thanks to the speed and daring of Cool Papa Bell. Bell walked and stole second. With two out Jud Wilson had an infield hit, and the amazing Bell dashed all the way home from second, just beating the throw from the first baseman. The East led 1–0.

The bottom of the ninth inning brought even more drama. Suttles smacked a triple for the West squad against Paige. Then with one out Red Parnell hit a hard line drive to deep right field. Jimmy Crutchfield, the small but sure-handed right fielder for the East, made the catch. Mule tagged up from third and took off for home as Crutchfield unleashed a terrific throw that arrived at the plate just as Suttles did. The East's catcher, Bill Perkins, slapped the tag on Suttles, who was called out, ending the game.[6]

The 1935 game was even more exciting. Negro League players still talk about it as one of the most memorable games of all time. For the game that year, the Crawfords were switched to the West squad. With Josh Gibson hitting fourth and Suttles fifth, the West had two of the Negro Leagues' biggest home-run hitters batting back-to-back.

Leading the East was the great Cuban ballplayer

Martin Dihigo. Dihigo was one of the best all-around players in the history of the game. He regularly hit over .300. In 1935, he tied Gibson for the Negro League home-run mark, and the following year he was the league's home-run champion. In addition to being a great fielder with a strong throwing arm, Dihigo was also a top pitcher. Because he spent much of his career playing in Cuba and Mexico, Dihigo's accomplishments are sometimes ignored, but he played for several years in the National Negro League for Alex Pompez's New York Cubans.

The 1935 East-West game was tied up 4–4 after nine innings. The West team was still in the game thanks to another remarkable fielding play by Jimmy Crutchfield. Crutchfield had won the East-West game the previous year by throwing out Suttles at the plate to end the game. In the top of the eighth of the 1935 game, with the score tied, Biz Mackey hit a line drive deep into right center field. Cool Papa Bell in center and Crutchfield in right took off in pursuit, but it looked as if the ball would travel between them. At the last second, Crutchfield stuck out his bare hand and caught the ball.

In the top of the tenth inning, the East scored four times to take an 8–4 lead, but amazingly, the West came back with four runs to tie the game again. Then, in the bottom of the eleventh, with Dihigo pitching, Cool Papa Bell walked. Dihigo got the next two batters out, but Bell advanced to second base. Josh Gibson had already slugged two doubles and a single, so Dihigo decided to walk him intentionally. Mule Suttles came up to bat. The count went to one ball and one strike, and Dihigo came in with a fastball. The huge Suttles swung hard and connected, sending the ball soaring to right center. The ball traveled up and up, and landed in the upper deck. It was a tremendous clout and ended the game. The

West were winners, 11–8. As Suttles rounded the bases, he was mobbed by his teammates and the overjoyed fans who poured onto the field.[7]

Some of the greatest crowds for the East-West games came in the years just before Jackie Robinson broke the Major League color barrier. By its final years, white sportswriters flocked to the annual game to watch the stars they had ignored during the rest of the year. The game became a proving ground for young Major League prospects. Robinson and his future Brooklyn Dodger teammate Roy Campanella showed off their talents at the East-West game. So did other future Major League stars such as Larry Doby, Jim Gilliam, Monte Irvin, and Joe Black.

For the older Negro Leaguers, the East-West game had a different meaning. It was their only opportunity to show off their talents to a large and appreciative audience. Because of their age and the strict quotas that sharply limited the number of blacks allowed into the Major Leagues, Willie Wells, Buck Leonard, and Cool Papa Bell would never get a chance to play Major League ball. For them, and for all of the Negro League All-Stars who were never given the chance to play in the majors, the East-West game would have to suffice as the one day each year when they received the recognition they deserved.

CRACKS IN THE WALL

The Major League owners, along with Commissioner Landis, were determined to keep their teams all-white, but in certain parts of the United States high-level integrated baseball flourished in the 1930s. Unlike today, during the 1930s and 1940s there were no Major League teams west of Chicago. Over half the nation never got to see Major League teams in their area. In many of these places, top semiprofessional teams developed apart from Major League baseball, and there was not always the absolute racial divide that existed in the majors.

The best racially integrated baseball team in the 1930s was based in the town of Bismarck, North Dakota. The rural sparsely populated state of North Dakota is the last place you would expect to find great black stars playing in the 1930s. Bismarck's mayor, Neil Churchill, who was also an auto dealer, hoped that putting together a successful baseball team would help promote the town, and he set out to sign the best players available.

In 1934, Quincy Troupe, one of the stars for the Chicago American Giants, joined the Bismarck team. The following year, Satchel Paige had a salary dispute with the Crawfords owner, Gus Greenlee. The recently married Paige wanted more money, saying that "after the honeymoon, I started noticing a powerful lightness in my hip pocket."[8] When the Bismarck club offered Paige $400 a month plus the right to hire himself out to other teams in the area, Paige could not resist. Ted "Double Duty" Radcliffe was also persuaded to travel out to North Dakota, and the Bismarck team suddenly was looking very fine indeed.

Unfortunately, Mayor Churchill's open-mindedness was not matched by all of the townspeople of Bismarck. When Paige and his wife, Toadalo, looked for a place to live, no one would rent to them. They ended up having to live in an abandoned railroad freight car.

The Bismarck team won ninety-five games and lost only five that year, playing against other professional teams in the region. Their top rival, Jamestown, as well as other Dakota teams, also hired Negro League players. None, however, could match Bismarck's.

When a touring group of Major League players led by all-time greats Jimmie Foxx and Heinie Manush traveled through Dakota, the Bismarck team beat them in three straight games. At the end of the season, the National Baseball Tournament was held in Wichita, Kansas. It was open to all teams, regardless of race, and the team that won would win $10,000. Negro League teams and top professional clubs from all over the Midwest and West entered the tournament. The Bismarck team had picked up two top Negro League pitchers, Hilton Smith and Chet Brewer, and along with Troupe, Paige, Radcliffe, and Moose Johnson, a big home-run hitter and probably the team's best white player, Bismarck could not be matched. The year 1935 was a glorious one for baseball in the Dakotas.

The Denver Post Tournament was probably the most prestigious of all. It was started in 1915 and attracted teams from all over the nation. In the 1930s, black teams began playing in the tournament. The 1936 Crawfords, which Paige had rejoined, won the tournament, earning $7,500 dollars. The following year a group of Negro League stars that included Josh Gibson, Cool Papa Bell, Paige, and pitcher Leroy Matlock played in the Dominican Republic. Upon their return to the United States, they went to Denver and won the tournament.

In addition to tournaments and the Bismarck team, integrated baseball was played in the California Winter League. There were no Major League teams in California until 1958, but California had a thriving winter league. Many Major Leaguers and Negro League players competed against each other on the West Coast.

Although blacks had proved themselves many times against Major League competition, the nation's leading black newspapers took the tournaments very seriously. Major Leaguers sometimes used the excuse that their games against Negro League players were only exhibitions. But no one could call the tournaments an exhibition—winning meant big money. The Negro League players' performance proved once again that black ballplayers could beat any team willing to play them.

The tournaments, the integrated Midwest teams, and the California league were also important because they provided many white fans with their first chance to get a sustained look at the top black players. It was becoming increasingly obvious to baseball fans that some of the best players in the world were black. Eventually, some of those fans would start to think about the injustice of blacks being excluded from the Major Leagues.

JOSH GIBSON

Nobody could hit a baseball harder or farther than Josh Gibson. For sixteen years, Gibson was the most feared batter in Negro League baseball. Gibson's talents were so remarkable that many tales arose about his tremendous power. One often-told story is that while playing for the Crawfords at Pittsburgh's Forbes Field in the 1930s, Josh hit a ball so high and far that no one saw it come down. The astonished umpire ruled Gibson's blast a home run. The next day, when the Crawfords were playing in Philadelphia, a ball suddenly dropped out of the sky and was caught by the surprised center fielder. The umpire from the previous day pointed at Gibson and shouted, "You're out!"

Josh Gibson was born in Buena Vista, Georgia, in 1911, the son of sharecropper farmers. When Gibson was a young boy, his father went to Pittsburgh to look for better work. After finding a job at a steel plant, Josh's father sent for the rest of the family. Young Josh Gibson was twelve years old when he joined his father in Pittsburgh. It was the boy's good fortune to move to a city that was becoming the black baseball capital of the United States.

By the age of sixteen, Gibson had reached his full growth. At six feet one inch (1.8 m), 215 pounds (97 kg), he had a powerful body with huge arms and a large chest. Gibson began playing as a catcher for black semiprofessional teams in the area. In Pittsburgh, word spread about his long-ball hitting. At the time, the Homestead Grays were the best team in black baseball, but they already had Buck Ewing and Vic Harris as catchers.

Gibson got his lucky break in 1930. The Kansas City Monarchs came to town to play the Grays. It was the best of the West against the best of the East, and Forbes Field was packed with over 30,000 fans. The Monarchs had introduced night baseball to America earlier that year, and they brought their portable light system with them for the game in Pittsburgh. Although the lighting was terrible by today's standards, fans poured into the stadium to see baseball played at night.

That night Smokey Joe Williams was pitching, and catcher Buck Ewing, unable to handle one of his pitches, injured his hand. Vic Harris was in the outfield, and the Grays manager and star third baseman Judy Johnson asked him to take over behind the plate. Harris refused, saying, "I'm not going to catch a game in candlelight, find somebody else." The panicked Johnson looked up in the stands and saw the eighteen-year-old Gibson. Josh jumped at the opportunity and finished the game. The Grays signed him to a contract, and Gibson was suddenly playing for the best black baseball team in America.

At the end of the 1930 season, the Grays faced off against John Henry Lloyd's Lincoln Giants in a nine-game series. The Grays had already beaten the Monarchs in eleven of twelve games that year, and the Giants were the only other serious competition left. During the series, the eighteen-year-old Gibson demonstrated that he was the biggest power hitter in all of baseball. In the first doubleheader between the two teams, Gibson slugged a ball over Forbes Field's center field wall, 457 feet (137 m) away. He was the first man ever to hit a ball over that fence. The teams then went to New York to continue the series at Yankee Stadium. The Grays were leading the series four games to two when Gibson hit one of the longest home runs in the history of Yankee Stadium. According to Judy Johnson, the ball Gibson hit traveled over the left field fence, over the back wall, and into the bull pen fence. The walls at Yankee Stadium have since been brought closer to the plate because home runs to that part of the park were so rare. Gibson's shot that day must have traveled over 500 feet (150 m). Babe Ruth, in all his years at Yankee Stadium, may never have hit a ball farther than the one the teenaged Gibson hit that day. The Grays won their series with the Lincoln Giants, and Gibson was a star.[9]

The following year, Gibson hit seventy-five home runs as the Grays barnstormed around the country. For Josh, though, the season was marred by tragedy. Gibson's wife, Helen, gave birth to twins but died in childbirth. Gibson was devastated. He was only nineteen years old, and he now had two children to raise. Since he spent most of the year on the road, Helen's family would have to do most of the child rearing.

The next year, Josh and most of his teammates left the Grays to play for Gus Greenlee's Pittsburgh Crawfords. Along with the great pitcher and showman Satchel Paige, the power-hitting Gibson was the Crawfords' main attraction. Josh's personality was very different from that of Paige. Josh was quiet and lacked Paige's charisma. But baseball fans still came to the ballpark to see one of Gibson's home runs.

Unlike most home-run hitters, Gibson had a short, compact swing. He was so strong and his bat speed so quick that he did not need a big swing. Josh was also unusual for a power hitter in that he hit to all fields. If the ball was inside, he would hit to left field; if it was outside, he would go with it and drive it to right.

Gibson was also a good fielding catcher. He had a strong arm for throwing out base runners, but he sometimes had problems catching foul pop-ups and wild pitches.

Gibson played for the Crawfords from 1934 to 1936, and he led the Negro National League in home runs all three years. Most of the Crawfords games were barnstorming, rather than league contests, and unfortunately there is no record of how many home runs Gibson actually hit during those years. According to his Crawford teammate Judy Johnson, however, Gibson never hit fewer than sixty home runs during each of his years with the Crawfords. The Crawfords played the New York Cubans in the Negro League world series in 1935. Paige was playing for Bismarck in 1935, but Leroy Matlock pitched well for Pittsburgh all year. In the final and deciding game of the series, the Cubans were leading 7–5 when Gibson and Oscar Charleston hit home runs. Then Bell got on base and scored, and the Crawfords were champions.

Paige, Gibson, and other Crawfords' stars spent 1937 playing in the Dominican Republic. When Gibson returned, he was sold to Cum Posey's Grays. The Grays were now playing half their home games in Washington, D.C., in Griffith Stadium, where the American League Washington Senators played; the other half were played at Forbes Field, home of the Pittsburgh Pirates. These were two of the largest parks in all of baseball and were a nightmare for home run hitters, but Gibson was not to be deterred.

Cum Posey had again put together a terrific team. Gus Greenlee, though, had fallen on hard times, and the great Pittsburgh Crawfords team went out of business after the 1938 season. The Homestead Grays had a powerful combination with Gibson batting third and the left-handed hitting first baseman Buck Leonard batting fourth. Gibson and Leonard are often compared to Yankees Babe Ruth and Lou Gehrig as the most dangerous one-two punch in the history of baseball. Leonard had worked nine years for the Atlantic Coast Railroad in North Carolina and played on a semiprofessional team called the Black Swans before making it into the Negro National League. He was a fine fielder and one of the most consistent hitters in the Negro Leagues.

Led by Gibson and Leonard, the Grays were once again the best team in baseball, winning the Negro National League pennant every year from 1937 to 1945.

Gibson had a spectacular year in 1939—the record books show that he hit a home run every five times he came to the plate, despite the fact that he was playing in parks where it was extremely difficult to hit *any* homers. The Washington Senators owner Clark Griffith used to watch Gibson in amazement when the Grays played in Washington. The Senators were the worst club in the American League, and Griffith must have wished that he could have had Gibson playing in a Senators uniform at Griffith Field.

According to his teammates, Gibson had acquired a taste for beer and began drinking heavily around this time. Although he was normally a gentle and friendly man, Gibson could become loud and violent when he drank. In later years, as his health declined, his drinking increased. On the field, though, Gibson was still getting better.

Some of Gibson's happiest days were spent playing winter ball in Puerto Rico. The life-style for a ballplayer on the island was not as grueling as back on the United States mainland. Games were usually played only on weekends, and there was not much travel. And while many baseball fans on the American mainland remained ignorant of his accomplishments, Josh was a hero in Puerto Rico. He was famous for the long home runs he hit out of San Juan's Escambron Stadium and into a group of palm trees, nearly 500 feet (150 m) from home plate. Gibson's admirers climbed the trees and placed bright markers everywhere Josh's clouts had disappeared. The markers would remain in the trees for many years. In 1941, his batting average an astounding .479, he was named the Puerto Rican league's Most Valuable Player, an award that did not exist in the Negro National League.

Gibson spent the entire 1941 summer season playing in Mexico. Cum Posey was paying Gibson only $500 a month, and when Josh received an offer of $800 a month to play south of the border he accepted.

Josh returned to the Grays in 1942 and continued to dominate the Negro Leagues, once again hitting more home runs than any other player. One day that year Clark Griffith invited Gibson and Buck Leonard to the Washington Senators' office. He told them he would love to have the two men on the team but said that it would cause too many problems. Gibson and Leonard never heard from Griffith again.

1943 was probably Gibson's greatest year on the field, but personally it was a difficult and distressing time. Early in the year Josh spent ten days in the hospital. Cum Posey said that Gibson had suffered a nervous breakdown. According to his family, Gibson was diagnosed with a brain tumor, but if that was the correct diagnosis he never told anyone else about it. Josh was in and out of Washington's St. Elizabeth mental hospital for much of the year, suffering from alcoholism and possible drug addiction. Sometimes Josh would be taken from the hospital for a ball game and returned afterward. On the road, Gibson would get in fights in bars. Once he climbed naked out onto a window ledge and threatened to jump.

In spite of his problems, the troubled Gibson somehow managed to play outstanding baseball. He hit .521 for the season, the highest average in the history of the league. Once again Gibson was the Negro National League home run leader. During one game at Griffith Stadium, Gibson hit three long home runs into left field. That same year Josh hit eleven home runs over the long left field fence of Griffith Stadium. The Grays only played there one or two times a week, but Gibson had more home runs to left field than the Washington Senators team and their American League opponents hit in that ballpark the entire year! The Grays won the Negro League championship in 1943, led on the field by their unhappy star Josh Gibson.

Gibson's fragile health improved only slightly, but he had great years once again in 1944 and 1945. In 1945, the Brooklyn Dodgers announced that they had signed Jackie Robinson to a minor league contract. Gibson was stunned. He had been the king of black baseball, but now everybody turned their attention to Robinson. How could the Major Leagues be looking to the young and unproven Robinson to become its first black player when they could have chosen the greatest hitter in the history of black baseball? Gibson was only thirty-three, and he was still hitting some of the longest shots in the game's history.

In the earliest days of organized professional
baseball during the nineteenth century,
not all teams were racially segregated. One
of the best African-American players was
Bud Fowler, shown here in 1885 with the
Keokuk, Iowa, team of the Western League.

Smokey Joe Williams was one of the greatest pitchers in black baseball. He is shown here in 1915 when he played with New York's Lincoln Giants, the best black ball club of the period.

People who saw him play argue that John Henry Lloyd was the finest short-stop ever to play the game. Lloyd is shown here during the 1918 season when he was the Brooklyn Royal Giants' player-manager.

Rube Foster (back row, fourth from left) is
pictured with his Chicago American Giants.
Foster was a top pitcher before becoming
manager of the American Giants. In 1920
Foster organized the Negro National League,
the first successful black league.

Cool Papa Bell played for the St. Louis Stars
during the 1920s. Pitcher Satchel Paige
said Bell was so fast that he could turn
off the light switch and jump into bed
before the light went off.

Harlem residents waiting in line to vote
in 1926. This New York neighborhood
was a center of African-American culture
during the 1920s, and several of the top
Negro League clubs came from New York.

From 1932 to 1936 the Pittsburgh Crawfords
were the best and most exciting team in the
Negro National League. During the Crawfords' first
season in 1932, player-manager Oscar Charleston
(standing) is shown with four of the Crawfords'
top players—(left to right) Rap Dixon,
Josh Gibson, Judy Johnson, and Jud Wilson.

The great Satchel Paige was the most famous player in the history of Negro League baseball. Here Paige eyes the batter carefully while pitching for the Kansas City Monarchs at Yankee Stadium.

National Semi-Pro Champions – 1935

In 1935 the Bismarck, North Dakota, club signed top black players and became one of the best clubs in baseball. Satchel Paige, standing in the center of the back row, was one of their top players.

The Homestead Grays were one of the best
and longest-lasting teams in black baseball.
Between 1937 and 1945 the Grays won the
Negro National League pennant for nine
years straight. During those years the
Grays played half of their home games in
Pittsburgh and the other half in Washington.

The Cuban star Martin Dihigo played all positions except for catcher and was a great hitter. He spent much of his career playing in Latin America but played several seasons with the New York Cubans of the Negro National League.

Nobody could hit a
ball harder or farther
than Josh Gibson.
The powerful Gibson
stands at the plate
awaiting the pitch.

Gibson is tagged out
at home during the
1944 annual East-West
Negro League All-Star
game at Chicago's
Comiskey Park.

First baseman Buck Leonard batted
after Josh Gibson when they played
together on the Homestead Grays. Gibson
and Leonard are sometimes compared to
the New York Yankees' Babe Ruth and
Lou Gehrig as the most dangerous one-two
slugging combination in the history of baseball.

In 1937 many of the top Negro League players went to the Dominican Republic. The top team was the Trujillo All-Stars, named after the country's dictator, President Rafael Trujillo. In this team photo, Josh Gibson is in the back row on the far left, Satchel Paige is in the middle row on the far right, and Cool Papa Bell is in the middle of the front row.

In 1947 Jackie Robinson became the first African-American to play Major League baseball in the twentieth century. Robinson was signed by the Brooklyn Dodgers' general manager Branch Rickey, who is shown here with Robinson.

Robinson, a great base stealer, steals home against the New York Giants in 1956.

Even after Robinson joined the Brooklyn Dodgers,
many older great black players were ignored by
Major League clubs. Ray Dandridge (left),
was one of the Negro Leagues' great third
basemen. This photo was taken when he was
playing for the minor league Minneapolis Millers
during the 1950 season. Dandridge was never
given the opportunity to play in the majors.
On the right is the very young Willie Mays,
and Dave Barnhill is seated in the middle.

Cool Papa Bell, one of only eleven Negro
League players who have been elected to
the Baseball Hall of Fame, holding a plaque
while talking about his playing days.
Cool Papa Bell died in St. Louis in 1991.

The Dodgers knew that the first man to break the Major Leagues' color barrier would need exceptional mental and emotional strength. Dealing with the constant pressure, the taunts and insults, would require someone with extraordinary reserve. Although Gibson was clearly the game's greatest hitter, Dodger general manager Branch Rickey did not think he was the best man to take on the task of integrating Major League baseball.

During 1946, Gibson was bothered by his bad knees. He managed to have another fine year hitting, but it was very difficult for him to catch behind the plate. At the end of the season a depressed Gibson continued drinking heavily. On January 19, 1947, Gibson went to his mother's house and told her he was not feeling well. He went to lie down and died shortly afterward.

The cause of Gibson's death is not clear. He was only thirty-six years old. Some of his teammates believe he died from brain cancer, and that this helps explain his behavior during the last years of his life. Others believe that he died of a stroke. Another possibility is that Gibson drank himself to death or that drugs were involved. According to his friend and former teammate Ted Page, Gibson died of a broken heart. Page said, "When the Dodgers signed Jackie Robinson, Josh knew it was over for him. He wasn't going to make the big leagues, and he knew that because of his health and bad knees his career with the Grays was about over. He didn't know what to do with his life. He had no options."[10]

Josh Gibson was gone. Because of the color of his skin he never had the chance to play Major League ball. Sadly, too few got to see him play and, as the Negro Leagues passed away, Gibson was quickly forgotten. It would take many years before Josh Gibson would get the attention he deserved.

IN A FOREIGN LAND

Baseball south of the border and in the Caribbean played an increasingly important role in the lives of many Negro Leaguers in the 1930s and 1940s. The top players spent their winters in Cuba and Puerto Rico. Baseball has been Cuba's most popular sport since the late 1800s, and the level of play in the Cuban league was exceptional. By the 1930s, Puerto Rico had also developed a winter league of very high quality.

Latin baseball was a passionate affair. If the fans were displeased, a player could expect to be pelted with oranges and lemons. On the other hand, a great hit or fielding play was rewarded handsomely. Fans would throw money onto the field when they were especially impressed with a player's performance. Cool Papa Bell remembers collecting $200 from delirious fans after hitting two inside-the-park home runs during a game in Mexico. Players in Cuba and Puerto Rico experienced similar treatment.

Most American blacks who played in Latin America have fond memories of their time there.

Many learned to speak Spanish, and a few even settled down and remained after their playing days were over. Outside the United States, black players did not face the constant racism they encountered back home. The teams in Latin America were integrated, and blacks could stay at the best hotels and eat anywhere they wanted. Only the best Negro League players were asked to play in Cuba, Puerto Rico, and later the Dominican Republic and Mexico. They were paid well, often earning more than they made in the United States.

The most extraordinary year for Negro Leaguers in Latin America was 1937 in the Dominican Republic, a nation with which African-American baseball players had little experience. Baseball in the Dominican Republic was serious business. The country was run by dictator Rafael Trujillo, a man who thought so much of himself that he renamed Santo Domingo, the Dominican Republic's capital, Ciudad Trujillo after himself.

The Dominican league was made up of three teams—Santiago, San Pedro de Marcoris, and Ciudad Trujillo. In 1937, the dictator decided that Ciudad Trujillo must win the Dominican baseball championship. His political opponents supported the other two teams.

Trujillo's baseball officials decided to bring in the Negro National League's best players to ensure victory. They first approached Satchel Paige. Paige had recently returned to the Pittsburgh Crawfords after pitching for Bismarck. The Crawfords were training in New Orleans when Trujillo's men approached him. Paige told them he wasn't interested, but when they showed him a suitcase filled with money, Satchel changed his mind.

Frederico Nina, one of Trujillo's men, followed the Crawfords back to Pittsburgh to try to sign up more players. Pittsburgh's player-manager Oscar Charleston realized that he was losing his team. After finding Nina in a hotel in town, Charleston grabbed him by the neck and demanded to know "why [he] didn't go into the white league" to take players. The Crawfords' owner, Gus Greenlee, managed to have Nina arrested, charged with conspiracy, and deported.

Greenlee, however, was having cash problems. Paige made a telephone call from the Dominican Republic and convinced Cool Papa Bell to join him. Bell came down and brought with him Josh Gibson, outfielder Sam Bankhead, and the Crawfords' other top pitcher, Leroy Matlock.

Pittsburgh's African-American community was shocked. The best black baseball team in the United States, perhaps the best baseball team in the entire world, no longer existed. Its major players had moved to another country.

When the Crawfords stepped off the plane in Ciudad Trujillo, they were greeted by soldiers carrying rifles and were escorted to a press conference at a government building. Here they were introduced to the nation. During the season, Trujillo had the players housed at a country club with a swimming pool and other luxuries but also with armed soldiers patrolling the premises. For much of the season, Bell, Paige, Gibson, Bankhead, and Matlock were kept under a sort of house arrest. Cool Papa Bell remembers:

They kept us under guard at a private club. There were men with guns around all the time.

We could leave the club only two days a week. I don't know if they were trying to protect us or to keep us from getting away. I do know that one of the guards told me, "If you don't win they're going to kill Trujillo."

I laughed and said, "They don't kill people over baseball games."

He didn't laugh. He looked me right in the eye and said, "Down here they will do it."[1]

Following the example of Ciudad Trujillo, the two other teams in the league also imported Negro League stars from the United States. Chet Brewer, one of black baseball's great pitchers, signed up to play for the Santiago team.

Once, after Ciudad Trujillo had lost an important game to Santiago, Bell and his teammates were confronted by angry soldiers. Shooting their rifles into the air, they said to the Negro League stars, "El Presidente doesn't lose!"

In the championship game, Paige faced off against Brewer. Before the game, Paige had been warned by one of Trujillo's men: "Please take my advice and win; if you lose you may never see America again." Brewer and the Santiago team led the game 3–2 going into the bottom of the seventh inning. Then, with Cool Papa Bell on second base, Sam Bankhead hit a two-run homer. Paige retired the final six Santiago batters and Ciudad Trujillo was victorious.[2]

After leaving the Dominican Republic, Paige and his Negro League teammates returned to the United States and entered the Denver Post tournament. Calling themselves the Trujillo All-Stars, they won the championship game 17–3 behind the pitching of Leroy Matlock.

Starting in 1938, Mexico became the most important Latin American country for the Negro League stars. Martin Dihigo, Cool Papa Bell, Josh Gibson, Buck Leonard, Willie Wells, Quincy Troupe, Sam Bankhead, Hilton Smith, and Ray Dandridge all spent seasons playing in Mexico. Roy Campanella and Monte Irvin, Negro League stars who went on to great careers in the Major Leagues after Jackie Robinson integrated baseball, also played in the Mexican League.

Cool Papa Bell played in Mexico from 1938 to 1941. He was with the Torreon club in 1940 and won the league batting title with an average of .437. The following year, Bill Wright, who had been a star for the Baltimore Elite Giants, won the Mexican batting title with a .390 average. (Wright enjoyed Mexico so much that he settled down there after his playing days were over.) Josh Gibson also had a memorable year in Mexico in 1941. Playing for the great Vera Cruz team, Gibson hit 33 home runs, had 134 runs batted in, and did it in only 94 games.

As teammates on Vera Cruz, Gibson had the great veteran shortstop Willie Wells and the star third baseman Ray Dandridge, both of whom had been starring for the Newark Eagles.

It was the money of Jorge Pasquel that lured the top Negro League stars to Mexico. Pasquel was the largest liquor importer in Mexico and was able to offer players salaries that the Negro League owners back in the United States were unable to meet. Several Negro League teams were badly hurt by the defections of their top players. Pasquel also raided the Major Leagues and signed a few of the best white players, including pitchers Sal Maglie and Max Lanier and catcher Mickey Owens.

Fearing that salaries would be driven up and their talent depleted, the Major Leagues passed a rule banning the so-called outlaw players from returning to the majors. The more loosely organized Negro Leagues were not able to take such an action; as a result, the black teams were hurt the most by the Mexican League raids.

For the Negro Leaguers, Mexico meant a chance to earn both money and respect. Of course, many of the players found the food strange, were unable to speak the language, and felt homesick, but continuing through the 1940s Mexico provided black players opportunities that did not exist in the United States. Willie Wells expressed the opinion of many of the black ballplayers in Mexico when he said, "We are heroes here . . . [while] in the United States everything I did was regulated by color. Well, here in Mexico I am a man."[3]

Many black Cubans came to the United States to play in the Negro Leagues. During the early days of black baseball, Christobel Torriente of Rube Foster's American Giants was one of the game's most feared long ball hitters. And fastball pitcher José Mendez was one of the early stars of the original Negro National League.

An important figure in the history of Negro Leagues baseball was Alessandro "Alex" Pompez. Pompez was a black Cuban-American born in Key West, Florida. The wealthy Pompez was a sports promoter and businessman whose base of operation was New York. He owned Dyckman's Oval, a baseball park in Harlem, and helped operate the numbers-running business of gangster Dutch Schultz. During the 1920s, he owned the Cuban Stars of the Eastern Colored League, and in the 1930s and 1940s, Pompez owned the New York Cubans in the Negro National League.[4]

The New York Cubans were comprised of both black Americans and blacks from the island of Cuba. Due to Pompez's connections in Havana, most of the top black Cuban players who came to the United States ended up on his team. The 1935 New York Cubans won the second half of the Negro National League split season, and faced off against the first-half winners, the Pittsburgh Crawfords, in a seven-game play-off. Pompez's team was led by the future Hall of Famer great, Martin Dihigo. Luis Tiant, whose son Luis Tiant, Jr., would later star in the Major Leagues, was a top pitcher for the Stars. The Stars led the Crawfords three games to one but Pittsburgh swept the final three games to become the 1935 Negro League champions.

In later years, third baseman Orestes Minoso, shortstop Silvio Garcia, and outfielder Tetelo Vargas would distinguish themselves playing for Pompez's team, but some of the New York Cubans' best players were black Americans such as pitchers Dave Barnhill and Pat Scantlebury and catcher Louis Louden.

While during the first half of the twentieth century Negro League ballplayers depended on playing abroad, in the 1950s Latin Americans began entering the Major Leagues in significant numbers. Many of these players could not be categorized easily as either white or black. As baseball began to slowly integrate after the 1947 season, Major League teams rushed to sign Latin players they would formerly have shunned.

Today, players from the Caribbean are a dominant force in baseball in the United States. The 1992 world champion Toronto Blue Jays were led by pitcher Juan Guzman and second baseman Manny Lee from the Dominican Republic, and second baseman Roberto Alomar and outfielder Candy Maldonado from Puerto Rico. Other top Major League stars from the Dominican Republic are Julio Franco, George Bell, Felix Jose, Ramon Martinez, Jose Rijo, and Jay Bell; from Puerto Rico, Ruben Sierra, Juan Gonzalez, Benito Santiago, and Sandy Alomar, Jr.; and from Cuba, Jose Canseco and Rafael Palmiero.

These players are helping to sustain interest and excitement in baseball in the United States, much as Cool Papa Bell, Josh Gibson, and Satchel Paige helped nurture the game in Latin America in the 1930s and 1940s.

NEW HORIZONS

The 1940s were good years for black baseball. Besides the Homestead Grays and Kansas City Monarchs, there were several other strong teams and many outstanding players.

In the Negro National League, the Baltimore Elite Giants were led by their catcher Roy Campanella. Campanella learned his craft from one of the great defensive catchers of the game, the veteran Raleigh "Biz" Mackey. Campanella joined the Negro Leagues at the age of seventeen. He played in the Negro Leagues for ten years before spending another ten playing Major League ball for the Brooklyn Dodgers. During his ten years with the Dodgers, Campanella hit 242 home runs, and the Dodgers won five pennants. The hard pace and high quality of the Negro Leagues prepared Campanella for the Major Leagues. There were many times in the 1940s when he played three games a day. After retiring, Campanella was elected to baseball's Hall of Fame in 1969.

Although he was a great hitter, Campanella

admits he was nowhere near Josh Gibson's equal with a bat. He was, however, the top defensive catcher in the Negro Leagues by the mid-1940s.

One of the top clubs of the period was the Newark Eagles. In 1946, after the Homestead Grays had won nine consecutive National Negro League pennants, Newark finally took the crown. The Newark team was owned by Effa Manley, a glamorous and beautiful woman who was one of the most powerful figures in black baseball. She owned the team with her husband, the numbers runner Abe Manley, but Effa was responsible for running all the business affairs of the Eagles.

The Newark Eagles had many stars in the 1940s. Shortstop Willie Wells and third baseman Ray Dandridge were great players. Opposing teams found it nearly impossible to hit a ball past them through the right side of the infield. Wells later moved to second base and started there in the 1945 East-West All-Star game. Wells had led the St. Louis Stars some twenty years earlier in the original National Negro League.

The hard-throwing Newark pitcher Leon Day was perhaps the best pitcher in Negro League ball after Satchel Paige. Day struck out eighteen men in a 1942 game against the Baltimore Elite Giants—a Negro League record. Max Manning was another top Newark pitcher. Manning was known as "Dr. Cyclops" because of the thick glasses he wore.

Outfielder Monte Irvin was one of the Negro League's top batters. The Homestead Grays, New York Black Yankees, and Eagles all wanted Irvin, and he signed with the Eagles in 1941. Most of the Negro League players thought Irvin would be the player to integrate Major League baseball. In 1946, he led the Negro League in batting with a .395 average. Monte Irvin joined the National League New York Giants in 1949. He and the Kansas City Monarchs' Hank Thompson were the first blacks to play for the Giants.

Just before the Major Leagues were integrated, pitcher Don Newcombe and long ball hitter Larry Doby starred for the Eagles. Doby would become the first black player in the American League, joining the Cleveland Indians in the middle of the 1947 season. Newcombe would follow Robinson to Brooklyn, joining the Dodgers in 1949.

Along with the Kansas City Monarchs, the Eagles were positioned as the top club in Negro League baseball when Jackie Robinson entered the Major Leagues.

The Negro American League was weaker than the Negro National League, but there were several fine teams in addition to the Monarchs. The Birmingham Black Barons and Cleveland Buckeyes had many good young players, but they were always in danger of losing their best talent to teams with more money. Many players from the South signed up with the Birmingham club before moving on to a more financially secure team.

The crowds for the East-West game in the mid-1940s showed the strong appeal of black baseball. In 1947, the year Jackie Robinson joined the Dodgers, over 48,000 fans went to Comiskey Park to see the annual game.

Another indication of black baseball's strength was the exhibition series that took place after the 1946 season. A team of Negro League stars organized by Satchel Paige played a series of games against a team of top Major League stars. Over 400,000 fans paid to get a chance to see the two squads face off.[1]

Black baseball was flourishing; very few could have guessed that the end was near for Negro League ball.

SETTING THE STAGE

The Negro Leagues were gaining more attention, and some began to question why blacks were kept out of the Major Leagues. Several leading white sportswriters began writing about the injustice of the Major Leagues' boycott of black talent. Black newspapers were also pushing hard for integrating the national pastime. Ric Roberts, sportswriter for the *Pittsburgh Courier* regularly demanded that blacks be given the chance to play in the Major Leagues. When Roberts interviewed Major League owners and players, he always pressed them to explain the exclusion of blacks from the game.

In New York City in the 1940s, Mayor Fiorello La Guardia formed an Anti-Discrimination Committee that started to put pressure on the New York Yankees, New York Giants, and Brooklyn Dodgers to integrate their clubs. La Guardia's stand demonstrated that segregation in baseball was becoming more and more controversial.

In spite of the rising pressure, Major League baseball's conservative owners did not seem interested in changing. Many owners were making a lot of money by renting their ballparks to the Negro League teams: the New York Cubans played at the New York Giants' Polo Grounds; the New York Black Yankees played at Yankee Stadium; and the Homestead Grays played at Forbes Field and Griffith Stadium. The Major League teams would take about 20 percent of the net receipts from the stadium gate for the Negro League games played in their ballparks. It was a comfortable and profitable arrangement. The owners realized that letting blacks into their league could eventually destroy the Negro League teams from which they were making money.

Some sportswriters continued to oppose integrating the game. A *Sporting News* article criticized blacks pushing for integration of the Major Leagues, saying that "they ought to concede their own people are now protected and that nothing is served by allowing agitators to make an issue of a question on which both sides prefer to be let alone."

Many Negro League players and owners assumed that were baseball to be integrated it would be done by allowing an entire black team into the Major Leagues. In 1945, the Boston Red Sox, under pressure from local politicians, agreed to try out three Negro League players—Jackie Robinson of the Kansas City Monarchs, Sam Jethroe of the Cleveland Buckeyes, and Marvin Williams of the Philadelphia Stars. The three performed impressively, but the Red Sox had no real intention of signing a black player and their "tryout" was quickly forgotten.

Change was made possible when Kenesaw Mountain Landis, who had been the commissioner of Major League baseball for twenty-five years, died in 1945. Landis had helped to keep the Major League game all white.

In 1943, when Bill Veeck agreed to buy the Philadelphia Phillies and sign Negro Leaguers to bolster the team's fortunes, Landis had intervened. It was World War II and blacks were fighting for their nation abroad. Veeck figured it was a good time to break the Major League color barrier. He planned to add Paige, Gibson, Buck Leonard, and Roy Campanella to the team. Veeck informed Landis of his intention and found out the next day that the Phillies owner had sold the team back to the National

League. The team was then sold to lumber dealer Bill Cox for a lot less than Veeck had agreed to pay.[2]

Landis was succeeded by Happy Chandler. Chandler, a southerner and the former governor of Kentucky, viewed the question of blacks in baseball very differently than Landis. Like many Americans, Chandler's thinking was deeply affected by World War II. Millions of young men, both black and white, had volunteered and risked their lives fighting in Europe and the Pacific. Many had not made it back to the United States. The new commissioner announced, "I've seen the bloody battlefields, and if black men can fight and die in Okinawa, Guadalcanal, and in the South Pacific, they can play baseball in America." Seeing that the time when blacks would be playing Major League ball was close at hand, the Brooklyn Dodgers general manager, Branch Rickey, sprang into action.

JACKIE

Branch Rickey had his scouts report to him on the top Negro League stars. Many of the best players were getting old. By 1945, Cool Papa Bell was forty-two years old, Satchel Paige was thirty-nine, and Josh Gibson was thirty-three. Rickey wanted a player on the rise, one who could play for the Dodgers for many years. He also knew that whoever he chose would have to be able to handle the pressures of being the first man to break baseball's color barrier. The Brooklyn scouts recommended Jackie Robinson.

Jackie Robinson was born on January 31, 1919, and grew up in a poor family in Pasadena, California. He was raised by his mother, who worked cleaning people's houses. The neighborhood Robinson grew up in was unusual in that it was integrated.

Robinson went on to college, attending the University of California at Los Angeles. He was a great collegiate athlete, especially in football, where he was voted onto the All-American team. He also played baseball and basketball. After college, Robinson spent three years in the army.

When Robinson left the service in 1944, he needed a job. During a Negro League game at Wrigley Field, he approached Kansas City Monarchs pitcher Hilton Smith, warming up in the bull pen. Robinson asked Smith if he could help him get a chance with the Monarchs. Smith spoke to the Kansas City owner, J. L. Wilkinson, and Robinson was invited to join the team as a rookie in 1945.[3]

Jackie started in 1945 as the Monarchs' shortstop. He had a fine year, hitting for an average of .345, and was the West team's shortstop for the annual East-West game.

Robinson was strong-willed and proud, and he did not get along well with many of his Monarchs teammates. He neither smoked nor drank, and while his teammates were out on the town, Robinson usually stayed behind in his hotel room.

During the 1945 season, rumors spread that Robinson would be signed to a Major League contract. Many of his teammates worried that the Negro League rookie was not the best candidate to represent them in the Major Leagues. Some of the older players, who had given their lives to the Negro Leagues, did not think it fair that a newcomer like Robinson should be chosen. Satchel Paige and Hilton Smith both believed that of all the Monarchs starting infielders in 1945, Robinson was the least polished. Cleveland Indians pitcher Bob Feller, who had faced off against Robinson during barnstorming games, stated that Robinson did not have the talent to make it in the Major Leagues. Others, like the Monarchs veteran second baseman Newt Allen, recognized Robinson's fine baserunning, hitting skill, and strong determination. Allen worried, however, that Robinson did not have the arm to play shortstop, and, in fact, Robinson would spend most of his Major League career at second and first. Buck Leonard has always said that the reason the Dodgers chose Robinson was because he had already played against whites in college at UCLA.

On August 28, 1945, Robinson was invited to meet with Rickey at the Dodgers' offices. Rickey's motives for inviting Robinson to that meeting are a matter of dispute. That year, Rickey had been involved in setting up a new baseball league for blacks, the United States Baseball League. One of the teams, the Brooklyn Brown Dodgers, would be run by the Dodgers and play out of their park in Ebbetts Field. The new league failed quickly, going out of business in a matter of months. When Rickey asked Robinson to sign a contract in 1945, was it so Robinson could join the Brooklyn Dodgers organization, or so that he could lead the Brooklyn Brown Dodgers? Bill Veeck thinks that it was only when the Brown Dodgers failed that Rickey decided to have Robinson join the Major League club. According to Rickey, the Brown Dodgers were used as a front so Rickey could scout black players who would eventually join the Major League team. Robinson supports Rickey's account.

At their meeting, Rickey described in detail to Robinson the insults that he would face from racist players, fans, and umpires if he did indeed play Major League ball. The Dodgers general manager assumed different personalities, playing the role of a racist room clerk at a hotel and then that of a bigoted waiter in a segregated restaurant. He asked Robinson how he would react to pitchers throwing at his head and base runners trying to injure him with their spikes.

Robinson asked the Dodgers general manager, "Mr. Rickey, do you want a ballplayer who's afraid to fight back?" Rickey shot back, "I want a player with guts enough *not* to fight back. You've got to do this job with base hits and stolen bases and fielding ground balls, Jackie. *Nothing else.*"

After their meeting, Robinson signed a contract with the Dodgers. In October, Rickey announced that Jackie Robinson would be joining the Dodgers top minor league team, the Montreal Royals, in the International League for the 1946 season.

The Montreal Royals had their spring training in Vero Beach, Florida. It was Robinson's first time in the South, and he was constantly reminded that under the law he was seen as a second-class citizen. Robinson could not stay in the same hotel as his white teammates and had to be put up by a local black family. When Robinson took a city bus, he had to ride in the back. That spring, Jackie spent all his time off the field with his wife, Rachel. Her support helped him through that difficult spring.

No black man had played in organized baseball, outside the Negro Leagues, in America in the twentieth century. So when Jackie Robinson stepped to the plate in 1946 for the Montreal Royals in a game against the Jersey City team, the entire baseball world took notice. In his first game, Robinson had four hits, including a home run, and stole two bases in leading the Royals to a 14–1 victory. Robinson endured racial taunts from the fans in several cities and handled the pressure of being a trailblazer gracefully. He led the International League in batting with a .349 average in 1946 and stole 40 bases.

Black sports fans followed Robinson's accomplishments with enthusiasm. Several other blacks joined minor league teams in 1946, most notably Roy Campanella and Don Newcombe. They were signed by the Dodgers and joined the team's Class-B minor league club in Nashua, New Hampshire.

Understandably, the major black newspapers used much of their space to report on these exciting new developments. The Negro League teams, however, were not neglected by the game's black fans. Crowds of over 10,000 were not uncommon for Negro League games in 1946. The Negro League owners worried about losing their best players, but it was a good year for most teams.

In April 1947, the Brooklyn Dodgers announced that Robinson would be spending the season with the Dodgers. Cool Papa Bell remembers that he cried for joy when he heard the news on the radio. Even though Robinson had few friends among the Negro League veterans, they all wished him well and had great respect for the courage he demonstrated under tremendous pressures.

1947 would be a very difficult year for Jackie Robinson. There were hate letters and death threats that Robinson received from racists who did not want to see a black man playing alongside whites.

Robinson even faced resistance from some of his own teammates. During spring training, a group of Dodgers players met to discuss a plan to refuse to take the field if Robinson played. Rickey called in the players involved and the revolt was quickly put down.

When the Dodgers played the Philadelphia Phillies, the Phillies taunted Robinson continuously. Shouts of "nigger" and "snowflake" came out of the Philadelphia dugout all through the game. The St. Louis Cardinals team tried to organize a boycott of their games with Brooklyn when Robinson and the Dodgers came into town. It was not until the National League President Ford Frick threatened the Cardinals with suspension that they agreed to play.

Robinson did not have much support from baseball's executives, either. In 1946, a secret report that called for maintaining segregation in baseball was supported by the owners fifteen to one. The Brooklyn team had cast the single dissenting vote.

Robinson triumphed in spite of all the abuse. In 1947 he hit .297, stole 29 bases, and led the club in runs scored with 125. With the help of their new star, the Dodgers won the National League pennant.

As Rickey had insisted, Robinson did not respond to the abuse and taunts aimed at him during 1947. After proving himself on the field that year, however, Robinson was determined to stand up for himself. From 1948 on, Robinson challenged anyone who showed him disrespect. In 1949, Jackie Robinson was the National League's Most Valuable Player, hitting .342 with 124 runs batted in. Robinson played for the Dodgers until 1956, and in six of those years Brooklyn won the National League pennant.

Robinson's great success would open the door to other blacks. No team that hoped to remain competitive could completely ignore the many Negro League stars hoping to get their chance in the Major Leagues. Baseball would never be the same again.

AFTER THE COLOR
BAR FELL

The African-American community followed Robinson's journey with great pride. In the nation's leading black newspapers, Robinson's performance was nearly always the lead sports story. The sixteen black ballplayers who had joined various minor league teams by 1947 were also big stories in the black newspapers. Up until 1946, the black presses' sports pages had focused on promoting the Negro Leagues and black baseball. The *Chicago Defender*, the *Pittsburgh Courier*, the Baltimore-based *Afro-American*, and New York's *Amsterdam News* all played an important role in building black baseball's popularity.

But black baseball suddenly took a backseat to the revolution occurring in the Major Leagues. Tremendous home runs by Josh Gibson were ignored, while newspapers looked at what Robinson was doing in Montreal. When Robinson made it to the Dodgers, the Negro Leaguers were largely forgotten. Thousands of black fans went to see Robinson play in whatever city he appeared. While formerly they might have bought tickets to see the Negro League teams in their communities, they now paid to see the Dodgers.

Except for the annual East-West game, the 1947 season was a tough year for Negro League teams. Crowds in many cities dwindled to under 2,000 a game, and most of the teams lost money.

In 1948 Satchel Paige joined the Cleveland Indians and Roy Campanella joined the Dodgers. It was a disastrous year for the Negro Leagues. At the end of the year, the Negro National League announced it was going out of business. The Homestead Grays and Newark Eagles, teams that had fielded terrific teams only two years earlier, had ceased to exist.

The Negro American League continued in existence until 1960, but after 1948 it was only a weak imitation of what it had once been. Teams played in small towns where professional baseball was rarely seen. And although a few very good young players signed on with Negro League clubs in the 1950s, as soon as their talents began to blossom they were quickly signed up by one of the Major League clubs.

Three of the greatest players in Major League history began their careers as young men in the Negro Leagues.

Hank Aaron was, like Satchel Paige, a native of Mobile, Alabama. Aaron was playing for the Mobile Bears, a black semiprofessional team, when the Indianapolis Clowns of the Negro American League came to town. The Clowns were impressed with Aaron and signed him. The eighteen-year-old Aaron spent part of 1952 with the Clowns before the National League Milwaukee Braves bought his contract. Aaron would go on to become the greatest home-run hitter in the history of the Major Leagues, hitting 755 round-trippers.

Willie Mays, who some regard as the best out-fielder in the history of the game, played as a teenager for the Birmingham Black Barons before going on to glory in the Major Leagues. Mays would later say, "The Major Leagues were easy for me. I learned baseball the hard way. The Negro Leagues made me."

Ernie Banks, after getting out of the army, played for the Kansas City Monarchs in 1953. Banks went on to become the top slugger in the history of the Chicago Cubs.

During their childhoods, Aaron, Mays, and Banks had all looked up to the Negro League stars. None of them had dreamed they would have the chance to play in the Major Leagues. Now all three are in the Hall of Fame.

As the fans lost interest, some of the surviving black teams resorted to carnivals and entertainment to try to keep the interest alive. The Indianapolis Clowns had a woman play second base for them one year, and used midgets to try to attract fans. The Clowns continued barnstorming until 1968 before going out of business. By then, blacks were firmly established in the Major Leagues.

The Negro Leagues were now history. Their success had in many respects ensured their eventual extinction. The Negro League teams had developed and nurtured great talent. They had provided a good living for hundreds of ballplayers and provided entertainment for millions. As social relations between the races improved, and overt racism began to recede, it became obvious that the Negro Leagues' many great ballplayers could help any Major League team willing to recruit them. The ability of the top black ball clubs to prosper finally led baseball's white establishment to recognize that black baseball fans were a valuable resource.

The passing away of the Negro Leagues as an

institution may be seen by some as unfortunate, but for black ballplayers the opportunity to play Major League ball was to be celebrated. Black baseball players would finally receive the recognition and respect they deserved from all of America. Rube Foster, the father of the Negro Leagues, had recognized the integration of baseball as his ultimate goal. Foster explained that one of the reasons he organized the National Negro League was so that when the white leagues decided to let blacks in, "we would be ready." Foster and his successors in the Negro Leagues accomplished what they had set out to do.

THOSE LEFT BEHIND

The integration of Major League baseball by Jackie Robinson in 1947 did not mean that the baseball establishment was suddenly going to welcome black ballplayers with open arms.

Most teams had strict quotas through the 1950s, quotas that limited the number of blacks each team had to two or three. While baseball was no longer segregated, racism still prevailed throughout the Major Leagues. In 1953, there were only twenty blacks playing Major League ball and they were on only seven of the sixteen teams. The Boston Red Sox did not have any black players until Elijah "Pumpsie" Green joined the team in 1959.

Many of the Negro Leagues' great stars were left behind. The Major League teams only seemed interested in the younger players. Cool Papa Bell, Buck Leonard, and Willie Wells were just ending their glorious careers when the Major League doors opened.

Buck O'Neil was thirty-five years old when Robinson joined the Dodgers. O'Neil hit .350 with the

Kansas City Monarchs in 1946, but he never got asked up to the Majors. O'Neil saw his Monarchs teammates—Jackie Robinson, Satchel Paige, Elston Howard, Hank Thompson, Ernie Banks, Connie Johnson, and Willard Brown—all signed by Major League teams. O'Neil stayed with the Monarchs, managing the team from 1947 until 1955, and later became a scout and a coach for the Chicago Cubs in the National League. Like most of the other Negro League players, O'Neil shows remarkably little bitterness about being denied the opportunity to get a shot at the Major Leagues. After his playing days were over, an interviewer asked O'Neil if he thought he had been born too soon. He replied,

Born too soon? Forget it. You forget that. Waste no tears for me. I had a beautiful life. I played with the greatest ballplayers in the world, and I played against the best ballplayers in the world. I saw this country and a lot of other countries, and I met some wonderful people. They say, "Buck, you were born at the wrong time." I say, "No, I was born right *on time."*[1]

The great Negro League pitcher Leon Day was thirty-one when Robinson debuted for the Dodgers. Larry Doby says, "I didn't see anybody in the Major Leagues that was better than Leon Day."[2] Day played in Mexico in 1947 and 1948 and returned to the Negro National League for 1949. He pitched well for minor league clubs after that, but was seen as too old to step up to the majors.

In the years that marked the demise of the Negro Leagues and the beginnings of integrated baseball, black ballplayer Ray Dandridge suffered the greatest injustice. Dandridge was short and bowlegged, stood about five feet seven inches tall (1.7 m) and did not look like an athlete, but he was the smoothest-fielding third baseman in all of baseball in the 1930s and 1940s. Dandridge could also hit. He regularly batted over .300, and it was almost impossible to get a fastball by him.

Dandridge starred for the Newark Eagles and also played for several years in Mexico. Then, in 1949, the National League New York Giants signed the thirty-five-year-old Dandridge to play for their top minor league team, the Minneapolis Millers. Dandridge batted .362 for the Millers and shone at third base. For some reason, the Giants did not bring Dandridge up to help their team. The Giants already had Monte Irvin and Hank Thompson, two former Negro League stars, on their roster. The club apparently decided another black ballplayer would have been one too many.

The next year Dandridge again starred for Minneapolis, and was voted the league's Most Valuable Player. The New York Giants were in a close pennant race that year and could have used Dandridge, but again they never called him up. The Giants finished third that year. If they had had Dandridge on their team, they might have been National League champions. Monte Irvin, who played for the Giants, blames the quota system for the team's failure to use Dandridge.

Dandridge was extremely popular in Minneapolis. He played there through the 1952 season, but he never got the chance to play in the Major Leagues. Dandridge said, "I just would have liked to have been up their one day, even if it was only to get a cup of coffee."

Dandridge and the older Negro League veterans still active in 1947 found themselves caught in a twilight zone. As the Negro Leagues crumbled, they found that they were unwanted. These men still had some good years of baseball left to play, but there was no place for them in organized baseball. While the Major League teams rushed to sign young black stars like Willie Mays and Ernie Banks, the Negro Leagues' older players were ignored and forgotten.

There is life after baseball, and after their playing days were over the Negro Leaguers went their various ways.

Oscar Charleston worked as a baggage handler at the Philadelphia railroad station; Cool Papa Bell became a security guard; Jimmy Crutchfield worked for twenty-five years in the post office; Buck Leonard sold real estate; Hilton Smith became a schoolteacher; and Judy Johnson became a scout for the Philadelphia A's and Philadelphia Phillies.

The Hall of Fame, Major League baseball, and the nation's newspapers ignored the story of the Negro Leagues, and its players had little more than memories.

Then, in 1966, Ted Williams, the last man to hit .400 in the Major Leagues, was voted into the Hall of Fame. During his induction speech, Williams criticized baseball's failure to recognize the great players of the Negro Leagues, and said, "I hope someday Satchel Paige and Josh Gibson will be voted into the Hall of Fame as symbols of the great Negro players who are not here only because they were not given the chance."

At long last, it seemed that the baseball world was waking up and was willing to recognize that a major part of baseball's history had been neglected. In 1971, Satchel Paige was elected to the Baseball Hall of Fame in Cooperstown, New York. Since then, ten other Negro League greats have joined Paige in the Hall of Fame: John Henry Lloyd, Rube Foster, Oscar Charleston, Martin Dihigo, Judy Johnson,

Cool Papa Bell, Josh Gibson, Buck Leonard, Monte Irvin, and Ray Dandridge.

There are many other Negro League stars who deserve induction into the Hall. Smokey Joe Williams, Biz Mackey, Bullet Joe Rogan, Leon Day, Willie Wells, and Mule Suttles are as deserving as many of the great white Major Leaguers who have been admitted to Cooperstown.

A recently formed organization, the Negro League Baseball Players Association, is working to bring attention to, and raise money for, surviving Negro League players. The association is trying to set up a permanent fund to help aging players. Unlike the major sports leagues today, which provide their players with generous pensions, the Negro League players receive nothing for the many years they spent playing baseball. It would take very little for today's Major League teams and its players, hundreds of whom are millionaires, to provide assistance to about 150 surviving Negro League players who were locked out of Major League baseball.

In 1991, the Negro League's Baseball Museum opened in Kansas City, Missouri. It is located only a few blocks from the YMCA where Rube Foster and other owners met to form the first Negro National League in 1920. The museum is dedicated to preserving and researching the story of black baseball in America.

Baseball has now been a vital part of this nation's social history for over 125 years. The story of the Negro Leagues helps us understand America as it was not very long ago. In spite of segregation, baseball thrived in black America during the first half of this century. The success of the Negro Leagues and of black baseball pushed organized baseball to integration long before many other institutions in America were ready to move in that direction. The pitcher

Don Newcombe remembers having dinner in his house in 1968 with the civil rights leader Martin Luther King, Jr., shortly before King's assassination. King told Newcombe, "You and Jackie and Roy will never know how easy you made it for me to do this job."[3]

Jackie Robinson's courage in integrating baseball shook the very foundation of racial segregation and inequality in America. The success of Robinson and those who followed him helped to serve as a constant reminder of the discrimination facing African-Americans in other walks of life. In the 1950s and 1960s, the civil rights movement would succeed in overturning laws that institutionalized racial segregation and denied blacks in the South the right to vote.

The Negro Leaguers' success made Robinson's breakthrough possible. In a very concrete sense, the Negro Leagues' triumphs contributed to changes that came decades later. The Negro Leaguers, however, did not see themselves as trailblazers. They were ballplayers, and the game was what mattered to them. The magic they performed on baseball diamonds around the world deserves to be remembered and treasured.

APPENDIX*

1920

Negro National League

Clubs were the Chicago American Giants, Chicago Giants, Cuban Stars, Dayton Marcos, Detroit Stars, Indianapolis ABCs, Kansas City Monarchs, and St. Louis Giants.

No final standings were published but the American Giants were awarded the pennant.

1921

Negro National League

	W	L	Pct.
Chicago American Giants	41	21	.661
Kansas City Monarchs	50	31	.617

* From Robert Peterson's *Only the Ball Was White*.

St. Louis Giants	33	23	.589
Detroit Stars	30	27	.526
Indianapolis ABCs	30	29	.508
Columbus Buckeyes	24	38	.387
Cincinnati (Cuban Stars)	23	39	.371
Chicago Giants	10	32	.239

1922

Negro National League

	W	L	Pct.
Chicago American Giants	36	23	.610
Indianapolis ABCs	46	33	.582
Detroit Stars	43	32	.573
Kansas City Monarchs	44	33	.571
St. Louis Stars	23	23	.500
Pittsburgh Keystones	16	21	.432
Cuban Stars	19	30	.388
Cleveland Tate Stars	17	29	.370

1923

Negro National League

	W	L	Pct.
Kansas City Monarchs	57	33	.633
Detroit Stars	40	27	.597
Chicago American Giants	41	29	.586
Indianapolis ABCs	45	34	.570
Cuban Stars (West)	27	31	.466
St. Louis Stars	23	31	.426
Toledo Tigers*	11	15	.423
Milwaukee Bears**	14	32	.304

* Disbanded July 15.
** Dropped in late season.

Eastern Colored League

	W	L	Pct.
Hilldale	32	17	.673
Cuban Stars (East)	23	17	.575
Brooklyn Royal Giants	18	18	.500
Bacharach Giants	19	23	.452
Lincoln Giants	16	22	.421
Baltimore Black Sox	19	30	.388

1924

Negro National League

	W	L	Pct.
Kansas City Monarchs	55	22	.714
Chicago American Giants	49	24	.671
Detroit Stars	37	27	.578
St. Louis Stars	40	36	.526
Birmingham Black Barons	32	37	.464
Memphis Red Sox*	29	37	.439
Cuban Stars (West)	16	33	.327
Cleveland Browns	15	34	.306

Eastern Colored League

	W	L	Pct.
Hilldale	47	22	.681
Baltimore Black Sox	30	19	.612
Lincoln Giants	31	25	.554
Bacharach Giants	30	29	.508
Harrisburg Giants	26	28	.481
Brooklyn Royal Giants	16	25	.390
Washington Potomacs	21	37	.362
Cuban Stars (East)	15	31	.326

* Succeeded Indianapolis ABCs, who started season in league.

1925

Negro National League

First Half

	W	L	Pct.
Kansas City Monarchs	31	9	.775
St. Louis Stars	31	14	.689
Detroit Stars	26	20	.565
Chicago American Giants	26	22	.542
Cuban Stars (West)	12	13	.480
Memphis Red Sox	18	24	.429
Indianapolis ABCs	13	24	.351
Birmingham Black Barons	14	33	.298

Second Half

	W	L	Pct.
St. Louis Stars	38	12	.760
Kansas City Monarchs	31	11	.738
Chicago American Giants	28	18	.609
Detroit Stars	27	20	.574
Cuban Stars (West)	10	12	.454
Birmingham Black Barons	10	16	.384
Memphis Red Sox	12	24	.333
Indianapolis ABCs	4	33	.108

Kansas City defeated St. Louis, four games to three, in a play-off for the league pennant.

Eastern Colored League

	W	L	Pct.
Hilldale	45	13	.775
Harrisburg Giants	37	18	.673
Baltimore Black Sox	31	19	.620
Bacharach Giants	26	26	.500

	W	L	Pct.
Brooklyn Royal Giants	13	20	.394
Cuban Stars (East)	15	26	.366
Lincoln Giants	7	39	.152

1926

Negro National League

First Half

	W	L	Pct.
Kansas City Monarchs	35	12	.745
Detroit Stars	33	17	.660
Chicago American Giants	28	16	.636
St. Louis Stars	29	18	.617
Indianapolis ABCs	28	18	.609
Cuban Stars (West)	6	27	.182
Dayton Marcos	7	32	.179
Cleveland Elites	5	32	.135

Second Half

	W	L	Pct.
Chicago American Giants	29	7	.806
Kansas City Monarchs	21	7	.750
St. Louis Stars	20	11	.645
Indianapolis ABCs	15	25	.375
Detroit Stars	13	23	.361
Cuban Stars (West)	10	20	.333

The American Giants defeated the Kansas City Monarchs, five games to four, in a play-off for the pennant. On the final day of the play-off, Willie Foster won both games of a doubleheader. Bullet Joe Rogan pitched both games for Kansas City.

Eastern Colored League

	W	L	Pct.
Bacharach Giants	34	20	.629
Harrisburg Giants	25	17	.595
Hilldale	34	24	.586
Cuban Stars (East)	28	21	.572
Lincoln Giants	19	22	.463
Baltimore Black Sox	18	29	.383
Brooklyn Royal Giants	7	20	.260
Newark Stars*	1	10	.091

1927

Negro National League

First Half

	W	L	Pct.
Chicago American Giants	32	14	.696
Kansas City Monarchs	36	18	.667
St. Louis Stars	32	19	.627
Detroit Stars	28	18	.609
Birmingham Black Barons	23	29	.442
Memphis Red Sox	19	25	.432
Cuban Stars (West)	15	23	.395
Cleveland Hornets	10	37	.213

Second Half

No final standings were published, but the Birmingham Black Barons were declared second-half winners.

The American Giants defeated the Black Barons in four straight play-off games to win the pennant.

* Disbanded in midseason.

Eastern Colored League

First Half

	W	L	Pct.
Bacharach Giants	29	17	.630
Baltimore Black Sox	23	17	.575
Cuban Stars (East)	24	19	.558
Harrisburg Giants	25	20	.556
Hilldale	17	28	.378
Brooklyn Royal Giants	10	21	.323

Second Half

	W	L	Pct.
Bacharach Giants	25	18	.581
Harrisburg Giants	16	12	.572
Hilldale	19	17	.528
Cuban Stars (East)	9	13	.409
Baltimore Black Sox	12	18	.400
Brooklyn Royal Giants	5	10	.333

1928

Negro National League

No final standings were published for either the first or second half. The St. Louis Stars were awarded the first-half championship, the Chicago American Giants the second.

Other clubs in the league were the Birmingham Black Barons, Cuban Stars (West), and Detroit Stars.

Eastern Colored League

The league broke up in late spring. Clubs were the Bacharach Giants, Baltimore Black Sox, Cuban Stars (East), Lincoln Giants, and Philadelphia Tigers.

1929

Negro National League

First Half

	W	L	Pct.
Kansas City Monarchs	28	11	.718
St. Louis Stars	28	14	.667
Detroit Stars	24	16	.600
Birmingham Black Barons	20	24	.454
Chicago American Giants	22	29	.431
Memphis Red Sox	14	22	.389
Cuban Stars (West)	6	14	.300

Second Half

	W	L	Pct.
Kansas City Monarchs	34	6	.850
Chicago American Giants	26	9	.743
St. Louis Stars	28	16	.636
Cuban Stars (West)	12	12	.500
Detroit Stars	10	23	.303
Birmingham Black Barons	9	27	.250
Memphis Red Sox	5	22	.185

American Negro League*

First Half

	W	L	Pct.
Baltimore Black Sox	24	11	.686
Lincoln Giants	22	11	.667
Homestead Grays	15	13	.536
Hilldale	15	20	.429
Bacharach Giants	11	20	.355
Cuban Stars (East)	6	16	.273

Second Half

	W	L	Pct.
Baltimore Black Sox	25	10	.714
Hilldale	24	15	.615
Lincoln Giants	18	15	.545
Homestead Grays	19	16	.543
Cuban Stars (East)	9	23	.281
Bacharach Giants	8	25	.242

1930

Negro National League

First Half

	W	L	Pct.
St. Louis Stars	41	15	.732
Kansas City Monarchs	31	14	.689
Memphis Red Sox	20	17	.541
Birmingham Black Barons	30	27	.526
Detroit Stars	26	26	.500
Cuban Stars (West)	17	23	.425
Chicago American Giants	24	39	.381
Nashville Elite Giants	13	35	.271

* The first use of this league title.

Second Half

	W	L	Pct.
Detroit Stars	24	7	.774
St. Louis Stars	22	7	.759
Chicago American Giants	19	12	.613
Kansas City Monarchs	8	12	.400
Nashville Elite Giants	7	12	.368
Cuban Stars (West)	6	12	.333
Memphis Red Sox	7	14	.333
Birmingham Black Barons	10	20	.333

The St. Louis Stars defeated the Detroit Stars in a play-off for the pennant.

1931

Negro National League

No final standings were published for either the first or second half, but the St. Louis Stars were declared winners of both. Other clubs were the Chicago American Giants, Cleveland Cubs, Detroit Stars, Indianapolis ABCs, and Louisville White Sox.

1933

Negro National League

First Half

	W	L	Pct.
Cole's American Giants (Chicago)	21	7	.750
Pittsburgh Crawfords	20	8	.714
Baltimore Black Sox	10	9	.526
Nashville Elite Giants	12	13	.480
Detroit Stars	13	20	.394
Columbus Blue Birds	11	18	.379

Second Half

The second-half schedule was not completed.

The American Giants claimed the pennant. Several months later, Gus Greenlee, league president, awarded the pennant to his club, the Pittsburgh Crawfords. This was disputed by the American Giants.

1934

Negro National League

First Half

	W	L	Pct.
Cole's American Giants (Chicago)	17	6	.739
Pittsburgh Crawfords	14	8	.636
Philadelphia Stars	12	9	.571
Newark Dodgers	6	5	.545
Nashville Elite Giants	9	11	.450
Cleveland Red Sox	2	22	.083

Second Half

	W	L	Pct.
Philadelphia Stars	11	4	.733
Nashville Elite Giants	6	3	.667
Pittsburgh Crawfords	15	9	.625
Cole's American Giants (Chicago)	11	9	.550
Cleveland Red Sox	2	3	.400
Newark Dodgers	5	9	.357
Bacharach Giants*	3	12	.200
Baltimore Black Sox*	1	6	.143

The Philadelphia Stars defeated Cole's American Giants, four games to three, in a play-off for the pennant.

* Added for second half.

1935

Negro National League

First Half

	W	L	Pct.
Pittsburgh Crawfords	26	6	.785
Columbus Elite Giants	17	11	.607
Homestead Grays	14	13	.519
Brooklyn Eagles	15	15	.500
Cole's American Giants (Chicago)	14	16	.467
Philadelphia Stars	14	17	.452
New York Cubans	10	16	.385
Newark Dodgers	8	20	.286

Second Half

	W	L	Pct.
New York Cubans	20	7	.741
Pittsburgh Crawfords	13	9	.591
Philadelphia Stars	14	10	.583
Columbus Elite Giants	10	10	.500
Homestead Grays	9	10	.474
Brooklyn Eagles	13	16	.448
Cole's American Giants (Chicago)	7	13	.350
Newark Dodgers	9	21	.300

The Pittsburgh Crawfords defeated the New York Cubans, four games to three, in a play-off for the pennant.

1936

Negro National League

First Half

	W	L	Pct.
Washington Elite Giants	14	10	.583
Philadelphia Stars	15	12	.556

Pittsburgh Crawfords	16	15	.516
Newark Eagles	15	18	.455
New York Cubans	9	11	.450
Homestead Grays	10	13	.435

Second Half

	W	L	Pct.
Pittsburgh Crawfords	20	9	.690
Newark Eagles	15	11	.577
New York Black Yankees	8	7	.533
New York Cubans	13	12	.520
Homestead Grays	12	14	.462
Philadelphia Stars	10	18	.357
Washington Elite Giants	7	14	.333

No play-off was held between the first- and second-half winners.

1937

Negro National League

First Half

	W	L	Pct.
Homestead Grays	21	9	.700
Newark Eagles	19	14	.576
Philadelphia Stars	12	11	.522
Washington Elite Giants	11	15	.423
Pittsburgh Crawfords	11	16	.407
New York Black Yankees	11	17	.393

Second Half

No final standings were published. The Homestead Grays were declared league champions.

Negro American League

First Half

	W	L	Pct.
Kansas City Monarchs	19	8	.704
Chicago American Giants	18	8	.692
Cincinnati Tigers	15	11	.577
Memphis Red Sox	13	13	.500
Detroit Stars	12	15	.444
Birmingham Black Barons	10	17	.370
Indianapolis Athletics	9	18	.333
St. Louis Stars	5	22	.185

Second Half

No final standings were published. However, the Kansas City Monarchs, first-half winners, defeated the Chicago American Giants in a series billed as a play-off, four games to one.

1938

Negro National League

First Half

	W	L	Pct.
Homestead Grays	26	6	.813
Philadelphia Stars	20	11	.645
Newark Eagles	11	11	.500
Pittsburgh Crawfords	14	14	.500
Baltimore Elite Giants	12	14	.462
New York Black Yankees	4	17	.190
Washington Black Senators	1	20	.048

Second Half

No final standings were published, but the league office announced that the teams finished in this order: Homestead, Philadelphia, Pittsburgh, Baltimore, Newark, and New York. The Washington club folded during the second half.

Negro American League

First Half*

	W	L	Pct.
Memphis Red Sox	21	4	.840
Kansas City Monarchs	19	5	.792
Indianapolis ABCs	6	6	.500
Atlanta Black Crackers	9	10	.474
Jacksonville Red Caps	3	4	.429
Chicago American Giants	8	13	.381
Birmingham Black Barons	3	11	.214

Second Half

	W	L	Pct.
Atlanta Black Crackers	12	4	.750
Chicago American Giants	17	7	.708
Kansas City Monarchs	13	10	.565
Indianapolis ABCs	8	13	.381
Memphis Red Sox	8	15	.348
Birmingham Black Barons	5	12	.294

* Not final; last published standings.

1939

Negro National League

	W	L	Pct.
Homestead Grays	33	14	.702
Newark Eagles	29	20	.592
Baltimore Elite Giants	25	21	.543
Philadelphia Stars	31	32	.492
New York Black Yankees	15	21	.417
New York Cubans	5	22	.185

To determine the champion, an elimination tourney was held among the top four teams. Baltimore defeated Newark in one series, and Homestead eliminated Philadelphia. Baltimore then beat Homestead, 2–0, and was declared the pennant winner.

Negro American League
First Half

	W	L	Pct.
Kansas City Monarchs	17	7	.708
Chicago American Giants	17	11	.607
Memphis Red Sox	11	11	.500
Cleveland Bears	9	9	.500
St. Louis Stars	10	12	.455

The Indianapolis ABCs dropped out of the league after a few games.

Second Half

No final standings were published. The Toledo Crawfords replaced the Indianapolis ABCs for the second half.

The Kansas City Monarchs were declared pennant winners after defeating the St. Louis Stars, three games to two, in a post-season series.

1940

Negro National League

	W	L	Pct.
Homestead Grays	28	13	.683
Baltimore Elite Giants	25	14	.641
Newark Eagles	25	17	.595
New York Cubans	12	19	.387
Philadelphia Stars	16	31	.340
New York Black Yankees	10	22	.313

Negro American League

First Half

	W	L	Pct.
Kansas City Monarchs	12	7	.632
Cleveland Bears	10	10	.500
Memphis Red Sox	12	12	.500
Birmingham Black Barons	9	9	.500
Chicago American Giants	9	15	.429
Indianapolis Crawfords	3	5	.375

Second Half

No final standings were published. The Kansas City Monarchs were declared pennant winners.

1941

Negro National League

First Half

	W	L	Pct.
Homestead Grays	17	9	.654
Newark Eagles	11	6	.647
Baltimore Elite Giants	13	10	.565
New York Cubans	7	10	.412

Philadelphia Stars	10	18	.357
New York Black Yankees	7	13	.350

Second Half

	W	L	Pct.
New York Cubans	4	2	.667
Newark Eagles	8	5	.615
Baltimore Elite Giants	9	8	.529
Homestead Grays	8	8	.500
New York Black Yankees	5	5	.500
Philadelphia Stars	2	8	.200

The Homestead Grays defeated the New York Cubans, three games to one, in a play-off for the pennant.

Negro American League

No final standings were published for either half of the split season. Clubs were Birmingham Black Barons, Chicago American Giants, Jacksonville Red Caps, Kansas City Monarchs, Memphis Red Sox, and New Orleans–St. Louis Stars.

In later years, the Monarchs were referred to as 1941 champions.

1942

Negro National League

	W	L	Pct.
Homestead Grays	21	11	.656
Baltimore Elite Giants	21	12	.636
Newark Eagles	18	16	.529
Philadelphia Stars	16	18	.471
New York Cubans	8	14	.364
New York Black Yankees	7	20	.259

Negro American League

No final standings were published for either half of the split season. The Kansas City Monarchs were declared winners of both halves. Other clubs were the Birmingham Black Barons, Chicago American Giants, Cincinnati Buckeyes, and Jacksonville Red Caps. The Red Caps dropped out in early July.

1943

Negro National League

First Half

	W	L	Pct.
Homestead Grays	17	4	.810
New York Cubans	13	6	.684
Harrisburg–St. Louis Stars*	5	4	.556
Newark Eagles	9	10	.474
Philadelphia Stars	11	16	.407
Baltimore Elite Giants	9	15	.375
New York Black Yankees	2	11	.154

Second Half

	W	L	Pct.
Homestead Grays	9	3	.750
Newark Eagles	9	4	.692
New York Cubans	4	3	.571
Baltimore Elite Giants	5	6	.455
Philadelphia Stars	7	9	.438
New York Black Yankees	0	10	.000

* Suspended when they withdrew to go on a barnstorming tour with a team headed by Dizzy Dean.

Negro American League

First Half

No final standings were published. The Birmingham Black Barons were declared winners.

Second Half

	W	L	Pct.
Chicago American Giants	13	5	.722
Birmingham Black Barons	5	3	.625
Cleveland Buckeyes	8	5	.615
Kansas City Monarchs	6	7	.462
Cincinnati Clowns	3	7	.300
Memphis Red Sox	4	11	.267

The Birmingham Black Barons defeated the Chicago American Giants, three games to two, in a play-off for the pennant.

1944

Negro National League

First Half

	W	L	Pct.
Homestead Grays	15	8	.652
Newark Eagles	13	9	.591
New York Cubans	12	10	.545
Baltimore Elite Giants	12	11	.522
Philadelphia Stars	7	11	.389
New York Black Yankees	2	13	.133

Second Half

	W	L	Pct.
Homestead Grays	12	4	.750
Philadelphia Stars	12	7	.632

	W	L	Pct.
Baltimore Elite Giants	12	9	.571
New York Cubans	4	4	.500
Newark Eagles	6	13	.316
New York Black Yankees	2	11	.154

Negro American League

First Half

	W	L	Pct.
Birmingham Black Barons	24	9	.727
Indianapolis–Cincinnati Clowns	18	13	.581
Cleveland Buckeyes	20	20	.500
Memphis Red Sox	20	23	.465
Kansas City Monarchs	12	19	.387
Chicago American Giants	10	20	.333

Second Half

	W	L	Pct.
Birmingham Black Barons	24	13	.649
Indianapolis–Cincinnati Clowns	22	18	.550
Chicago American Giants	22	19	.537
Cleveland Buckeyes	20	21	.488
Memphis Red Sox	24	28	.462
Kansas City Monarchs	11	23	.324

1945

Negro National League

First Half

	W	L	Pct.
Homestead Grays	18	7	.720
Philadelphia Stars	14	9	.609
Baltimore Elite Giants	13	9	.591

	W	L	Pct.
Newark Eagles	11	9	.550
New York Cubans	3	11	.214
New York Black Yankees	2	16	.111

Second Half

	W	L	Pct.
Homestead Grays	14	6	.700
Baltimore Elite Giants	12	8	.600
Newark Eagles	10	8	.556
Philadelphia Stars	7	10	.412
New York Black Yankees	5	10	.333
New York Cubans	3	9	.250

Negro American League

First Half

	W	L	Pct.
Cleveland Buckeyes	31	9	.775
Birmingham Black Barons	26	11	.703
Kansas City Monarchs	17	18	.486
Chicago American Giants	17	24	.415
Cincinnati Clowns	15	26	.366
Memphis Red Sox	13	31	.295

Second Half

	W	L	Pct.
Cleveland Buckeyes	22	7	.759
Chicago American Giants	22	11	.667
Kansas City Monarchs	15	12	.556
Cincinnati Clowns	15	13	.536
Birmingham Black Barons	13	19	.406
Memphis Red Sox	4	30	.118

1946

Negro National League
First Half

	W	L	Pct.
Newark Eagles	25	9	.735
Philadelphia Stars	17	12	.586
Homestead Grays	18	15	.545
New York Cubans	13	13	.500
Baltimore Elite Giants	14	17	.451
New York Black Yankees	3	24	.111

Second Half

	W	L	Pct.
Newark Eagles	22	7	.759
New York Cubans	15	8	.652
Baltimore Elite Giants	14	14	.500
Homestead Grays	9	13	.409
Philadelphia Stars	10	17	.370
New York Black Yankees	5	16	.238

Negro American League
First Half

	W	L	Pct.
Kansas City Monarchs	27	8	.771
Birmingham Black Barons	22	15	.595
Cleveland Buckeyes	14	17	.452
Indianapolis Clowns	15	19	.441
Memphis Red Sox	16	21	.432
Chicago American Giants	14	28	.333

Second Half

No final standings were published. The Kansas City Monarchs were declared winners.

1947

Negro National League

First Half

	W	L	Pct.
Newark Eagles	27	15	.643
New York Cubans	20	12	.625
Baltimore Elite Giants	23	20	.535
Homestead Grays	19	20	.487
Philadelphia Stars	13	16	.448
New York Black Yankees	6	25	.193

Second Half

No final standings were published. There was no play-off and the New York Cubans were awarded the pennant because they were said to have the best record for the full season.

Negro American League

No final standings were published for either the first or second half. The Cleveland Buckeyes were declared pennant winners. Other clubs were the Birmingham Black Barons, Chicago American Giants, Indianapolis Clowns, Kansas City Monarchs, and Memphis Red Sox.

1948

Negro National League

No final standings were published for either half of the split season. The Baltimore Elite Giants won the first-half championship and the Homestead Grays the second half. The Grays won three straight in a play-off for the title. Other clubs were the Newark Eagles, New York Black Yankees, New York Cubans, and Philadelphia Stars.

Negro American League

First Half

No final standings were published. The Birmingham Black Barons were declared winners.

Second Half

	W	L	Pct.
Kansas City Monarchs	19	7	.731
Birmingham Black Barons	17	7	.708
Memphis Red Sox	20	15	.571
Indianapolis Clowns	7	13	.350
Cleveland Buckeyes	10	21	.323
Chicago American Giants	7	17	.292

The Birmingham Black Barons defeated the Kansas City Monarchs, four games to three, in a play-off for the pennant.

1949

Negro American League

Eastern Division

First Half

	W	L	Pct.
Baltimore Elite Giants	24	12	.667
New York Cubans	14	10	.583
Philadelphia Stars	13	20	.394
Indianapolis Clowns	14	23	.378
Louisville Buckeyes	8	29	.216

Second Half

No final standings were published. The Baltimore Elite Giants were declared winners.

Western Division

No final standings were published for either half of the split season. In the first half, the order of finish was: Kansas City Monarchs, Chicago American Giants, Birmingham Black Barons, Houston Eagles, and Memphis Red Sox. For the second half, the Chicago American Giants, with a record of twenty-three wins and fifteen losses, were declared winners.

Kansas City, first-half champion, declined to meet the American Giants in a divisional-championship series because several of the Monarchs' best players had gone into organized ball during the season. The American Giants were therefore named Western Division champions. The Baltimore Elite Giants defeated the Chicago American Giants in four straight games for the league title.

1950

Negro American League

Eastern Division

First Half

	W	L	Pct.
Indianapolis Clowns	27	16	.628
Baltimore Elite Giants	10	9	.526
New York Cubans	12	13	.480
Philadelphia Stars	9	19	.321
Cleveland Buckeyes*	3	33	.083

* Disbanded at end of first half.

Second Half

	W	L	Pct.
New York Cubans	6	2	.750
Baltimore Elite Giants	14	11	.560
Indianapolis Clowns	18	21	.462
Philadelphia Stars	5	7	.417

Although finishing third, the Indianapolis Clowns were awarded the second-half championship because of a league ruling that the champion must play at least thirty games in a half.

Western Division

First Half

	W	L	Pct.
Kansas City Monarchs	30	11	.732
Birmingham Black Barons	38	14	.731
Houston Eagles	17	20	.459
Chicago American Giants	13	16	.448
Memphis Red Sox	11	19	.367

Second Half

	W	L	Pct.
Kansas City Monarchs	21	9	.700
Memphis Red Sox	18	8	.692
Birmingham Black Barons	13	10	.565
Houston Eagles	5	17	.227
Chicago American Giants	1	14	.067

No play-off was held between the divisional champions for the league title.

SOURCE NOTES

Chapter One

1. Robert Peterson, *Only the Ball Was White* (New Jersey: Prentice-Hall, 1970), p. 41.
2. Ibid., pp. 54–57.
3. Ibid., p. 79.
4. John B. Holway, *Blackball Stars: Negro League Pioneers* (New York: Carroll and Graf, 1992), pp. 37–38.
5. Ibid., p. 11.
6. Ibid., p. 12.
7. Ibid., p. 30.
8. Stephen Banker, *Black Diamonds: An Oral History of Negro Baseball* (Washington, D.C.: Tapes for Readers, 1992).

Chapter Two

1. James Bankes, *The Pittsburgh Crawfords: The Lives and Times of Baseball's Most Exciting Team* (Dubuque, Iowa: William C. Brown Publishers, 1991), p. 73.
2. John B. Holway, *Blackball Stars: Negro League Pioneers* (New York: Carroll and Graf, 1992), pp. 176–78.
3. James Bankes, *The Pittsburgh Crawfords: The Lives and Times of Baseball's Most Exciting Team* (Du-

buque, Iowa: William C. Brown Publishers, 1991), pp. 20–21.

4. Stephen Banker, *Black Diamonds: An Oral History of Negro Baseball* (Washington, D.C.: Tapes for Readers, 1992).

5. John B. Holway, *Blackball Stars: Negro League Pioneers* (New York: Carroll and Graf, 1992), pp. 301–2.

6. Donn Rogosin, *Invisible Men: Life in Baseball's Negro Leagues* (New York: Atheneum, 1983), pp. 141–51. For more on comedy and clowning in black baseball.

Chapter Three

1. John B. Holway, *Black Diamonds: Life in the Negro Leagues from the Men Who Lived It* (New York: Stadium Books, 1991), p. 98.

2. John B. Holway, *Josh and Satch: The Life and Times of Josh Gibson and Satchel Paige* (New York: Carroll and Graf, 1992), pp. 56–57.

3. Donn Rogosin, *Invisible Men: Life in Baseball's Negro Leagues* (New York: Atheneum, 1983), pp. 97–99. For one version of this oft-told story.

4. John B. Holway, *Josh and Satch: The Life and Times of Josh Gibson and Satchel Paige* (New York: Carroll and Graf, 1992), pp. 197–205.

5. Stephen Banker, *Black Diamonds: An Oral History of Negro Baseball* (Washington, D.C.: Tapes for Readers, 1992).

6. James Bankes, *The Pittsburgh Crawfords: The Lives and Times of Baseball's Most Exciting Team* (Dubuque, Iowa: William C. Brown Publishers, 1991), pp. 117–18.

7. Ibid., pp. 118–21.

8. John B. Holway, *Josh and Satch: The Life and Times of Josh Gibson and Satchel Paige* (New York: Carroll and Graf, 1992), p. 75.

9. Ibid., pp. 28–35.

10. James Bankes, *The Pittsburgh Crawfords: The Lives and Times of Baseball's Most Exciting Team* (Dubuque, Iowa: William C. Brown Publishers, 1991), p. 56.

Chapter Four

1. James Bankes, *The Pittsburgh Crawfords: The Lives and Times of Baseball's Most Exciting Team* (Dubuque, Iowa: William C. Brown Publishers, 1991), p. 129.
2. Ibid., p. 131.
3. Donn Rogosin, *Invisible Men: Life in Baseball's Negro Leagues* (New York: Atheneum, 1983), p. 172.
4. Ibid., pp. 110–13.

Chapter Five

1. Donn Rogosin, *Invisible Men: Life in Baseball's Negro Leagues* (New York: Atheneum, 1983), pp. 124–25.
2. Stephen Banker, *Black Diamonds: An Oral History of Negro Baseball* (Washington, D.C.: Tapes for Readers, 1992).
3. Donn Rogosin, *Invisible Men: Life in Baseball's Negro Leagues* (New York: Atheneum, 1983), pp. 201–2.

Chapter Six

1. John B. Holway, *Black Diamonds: Life in the Negro Leagues from the Men Who Lived It* (New York: Stadium Books, 1991), p. 104.
2. John B. Holway, *Blackball Stars: Negro League Pioneers* (New York: Carroll and Graf, 1992), p. 344.
3. Art Rust, Jr., *Get That Nigger Off the Field: The Oral History of the Negro Leagues* (Brooklyn, N.Y.: Bookmail Services, 1992), p. 119.

BIBLIOGRAPHY

Aaron, Henry, and Lonnie Wheeler. *I Had A Hammer: The Hank Aaron Story*. New York: HarperCollins, 1991.

Banker, Stephen. *Black Diamonds: An Oral History of Negro Baseball*. Washington, D.C.: Tapes for Readers, 1992.

Bankes, James. *The Pittsburgh Crawfords: The Lives and Times of Black Baseball's Most Exciting Team*. Dubuque, Iowa: William C. Brown, 1991.

Brashler, William. *Josh Gibson: A Life in the Negro Leagues*. New York: Harper & Row, 1978.

Dixon, Phil, and Patrick Hannigan. *The Negro Baseball Leagues: A Photographic History*. Mattituck, New York: Amereon House, 1992.

Holway, John B. *Black Diamonds: Life in the Negro Leagues from the Men Who Lived It*. New York: Stadium Books, 1991.

_____. *Blackball Stars: Negro League Pioneers*. New York: Carroll and Graf, 1992.

_____. *Josh and Satch: The Life and Times of Josh Gibson and Satchel Paige*. New York: Carroll and Graf, 1992.

Peterson, Robert. *Only the Ball Was White*. Englewood Cliffs, N.J.: Prentice Hall, 1970 (out of print).

Rogosin, Donn. *Invisible Men: Life in Baseball's Negro Leagues*. New York: Atheneum, 1983.

Rust, Art, Jr. *Get That Nigger Off The Field*. Brooklyn, N.Y.: Bookmail Services, 1992.

White, Sol. *Sol White's Official Baseball Guide*. Columbia, Mo.: Camden House (reprint of 1907 original).

INDEX

Aaron, H., 85
Afro-American, 84
Allen, N., 80
All-star games, 46–47,
  51, 52–55, insert 11
Amer. Association
  (1884), 12
Amer. Giants, 25, 49
Amer. Negro League,
  38
Amsterdam News, 84
Anson, C., 12–13

Bacharach Giants, 25,
  26, 33–34
Baltimore Black Sox,
  26, 43
Baltimore Elite Giants,
  50, 73
Bankhead, S., 68, 69
Banks, E., 86, 88

Barnhill, D., 72, insert
  15
Bell, J., 31, 42, 52, 53,
  54, 55, 57, 68, 69, 70,
  78, 82, 87, 90, 91,
  inserts 4, 13, 16
Birmingham Black
  Barons, 43, 50, 75, 86
Bismarck (N. Dak.)
  team, 56–57, insert 8
Black, J., 55
Black Swans, 62
Black world series, 27–
  28
Bolen, E., 27
Boudreau, L., 48
Brewer, C., 57, 69
Bklyn. Brown Dodgers,
  80
Bklyn. Royal Giants, 26,
  insert 2

Brown, W., 88
Buffalo Bisons, 13

California Winter
  League, 57
Campanella, R., 55, 73,
  82, 85
Chandler, H., 78
Charleston, O., 25–26,
  40, 52, 61, 68, 90,
  insert 6
Chattanooga team, 30
Chi. Amer. Giants, 19,
  21, 25, 28, 30–31, 34,
  insert 3
Chi. black baseball, 19–
  23
Chi. Defender, 24, 51, 84
Chi. Union Giants, 19
Churchill, N., 56
Ciudad Trujillo team,
  67
Cleveland Buckeyes, 75
Cobb, T., 18–19
Cole, R., 49
Comiskey, C., 15, 21
Cox, B., 78
Crutchfield, J., 41, 52,
  53, 54, 90
Cuba, 17–19, 66
Cuban Giants, 14, 20
Cuban Stars, 25, 50, 71

Dandridge, R., 69, 70,
  74, 88–89, 91, insert
  15
Day, L., 74, 75, 88, 91

Dayton, Marcos, 25
Dean, D., 46
Demoss, B., 23
Denver Post
  Tournament, 57
Det. Stars, 25, 28
Dihigo, M., 54, 69, 71,
  90, insert 10
Dixon, R., insert 6
Doby, L., 55, 88
Dominican Republic, 36,
  61, 67, 72
Dougherty, P., 21

East. Colored League,
  26–27, 33, 37, 38, 71
East. League, 12
Ewing, B., 59

Feller, B., 46, 79
Foster, A., 19–23, 24,
  insert 3
Foster, W., 52
Fowler, B., 12, insert 1
Foxx, J., 57
Frick, F., 83

Garcia, S., 72
Gibson, J., 40, 42, 45–46,
  52, 53, 54, 57, 58–65,
  68, 69, 70, 78, 84, 90,
  91, inserts 6, 11, 13
Gilliam, J., 55
Grant, F., 12, 13, 14
Green, E., 87
Greenlee, G., 40–42, 51,
  68

Griffith, C., 63
Grove, L., 26

Hall of Fame, 49, 73, 86, 90
Harlem, insert 5
Harris, V., 59
Havana Reds, 18
Hilldale Athletics, 25, 26, 27, 28
Homestead Grays, 32, 33, 34, 40, 49, 59–60, inserts, 9, 12
House of Colored Baseball (White), 14
Howard, E., 88

Ind. ABCs, 19, 25
Ind. Clowns, 36, 85, 86
Integrated baseball, 56–58, 67, 91–92
Internat'l League, 12, 81
Irwin, M., 55, 69, 74–75, 89, 91

Japan, 36
Jersey City team, 12
Jethroe, S., 77
Johnson, C., 88
Johnson, G., 21
Johnson, J., 27, 35, 40, 42, 59, 60, 61, 90, insert 6
Johnson, M., 57
Johnson, W., 26

K. C. Monarchs, 25, 27, 34–35, 36, 50, 75, 79, 86, insert 7
Keokuk team, insert 2
King, M.L., Jr., 92

LaGuardia, F., 76
Landis, K. M., 28, 55, 77
Lanier, Max, 70
Latin America, 36, 66–72
Leland Giants, 19, 21
Leonard, B., 45, 55, 62, 69, 80, 87, 91, insert 12
Lincoln Giants, 16, 26, 60, insert 2
Lloyd, J. H., 16–17, 18–19, 90, insert 2
Lundy, D., 34
Luque, A., 19

McGraw, J., 15, 21
Mackey, R., 27, 36, 54, 73, 91
Maglie, S., 70
Malarcher, D., 23, 30–31, 52
Manley, A., 74
Manley, E., 74
Manning, Max, 74
Manush, H., 57
Marcelle, O., 34
Mathewson, C., 21
Matlock, L., 57, 61, 68, 69
Mays, W., 86, insert 15

Mendez, J., 19, 28, 71
Mexico, 36, 63, 69, 70, 88, 89, 100
Minneapolis Millers, 89, insert 15
Minoso, O., 72
Mobile Bears, 85
Mobile Tigers, 43

Nat'l Negro League (second), 42
Negro Amer. League, 50, 75, 85
Negro League Baseball Players Association, 91
Negro Nat'l League, 25, 38, 71
Newark Eagles, 50, 70, 74–75, 85, 89
Newark team (1887), 12–13
Newcombe, D., 75, 82, 92
N.Y. Black Yankees, 50
N.Y. Cubans, 54, 71, insert 10
Nina, F., 67–68
N.W. League, 12

O'Neil, B., 44, 45, 87–88
Owens, M., 70

Page, T., 36, 42, 65
Paige, S., 30, 31, 35, 41, 42–49, 56, 57, 67, 69, 75, 78, 79, 85, 88, 90, inserts 4, 7, 8, 13
Paige, T., 56
Parnell, R., 53
Pasquel, J., 70
Perkins, B., 53
Petway, B., 18, 21
Phila. Giants, 15, 20–21
Phila. Stars, 50
Pittsburgh Courier, 51, 76, 84
Pgh. Crawfords, 26, 32, 41, 43, 57, 62, insert 6
Poles, S., 16
Pompez, A., 27, 54, 71
Posey, C., 33, 49
Puerto Rico, 36, 63, 66, 67, 72

Race riots, 24
Racial prejudice, 11, 29, 35, 55, 65, 77, 80, 82, 87
Racketeers, 41, 49–50, 74
Radcliffe, T., 42, 52–53, 56, 57
Redding, D., 16
Rickey, B., 52, 65, 78–83 passim, insert 14
Roberts, R., 76
Robinson, J., 14, 47, 55, 64, 77, 78–83, 88, insert 14
Robinson, R., 81
Rogan, J., 27, 91
Ruth, B., 16, 51, 60

St. Louis Stars, 25, 31,
74, insert 4
San Pedro de Marcoris
team, 67
Santiago team, 67
Santop, L., 16
Scales, G., 33
Scantlebury, P., 72
Schultz, D., 71
Shorling, J., 21
Smith, H., 45, 47, 57, 69,
79, 90
S. Negro League, 30
Sporting News, 13, 47,
77
Stearnes, T., 52, 53
Stillwater team, 12
Stovey, G., 12
Streeter, S., 33, 41
Suttles, M., 32, 52, 53,
54, 91

Thompson, H., 75, 88, 89
Tiant, L., 71–72
Tiant, L., Jr., 72
Toledo team, 12
Torreon team, 70

Torriente, C., 23, 71
Troupe, Q., 56, 57, 69
Trujillo All-Stars, 69,
insert 13

U. S. Baseball League,
80

Vargas, T., 72
Veeck, B., 47, 77
Vera Cruz team, 70

Waddell, R., 20
Wagner, H., 16
Walker, M., 12
Wells, W., 32–33, 52,
53, 55, 69, 70, 71, 74,
87, 91
White, S., 14, 15, 20
Wilkinson, J., 25, 47, 50,
79
Williams, J., 16, 33, 59,
91, insert 2
Williams, M., 77
Williams, T., 90
Wilson, J., 53, insert 6
Wright, B., 70